Managing Web-Based Customer Experiences

"Self-Service Integrated with Assisted-Service"

by

Dr. Jon Anton
Purdue University
Director of Benchmark Research
Center for Customer-Driven Quality

and

Mike Murphy
President and CEO
InQuira, Inc.

Content Editor
Anita Rockwell
Director of Business Intelligence
BenchmarkPortal, Inc.

Technical Writer
Cory Gideon Gunderson

Business Navigation

Only two centuries ago, early explorers (adventurous business executives of those bygone days) were guided primarily with a compass and celestial navigation using reference points like the North Star. Today's busy executive also needs guidance systems with just-in-time business intelligence to navigate through the challenges of locating, recruiting, keeping, and growing profitable customers. The Anton Press provides this navigational system through practical, how-to-do-it books for the modern day business executive.

ISBN 0-9719652-4-2

Dedication

This book is dedicated to every customer who's ever had to cool their heels in a service phone queue, or visit a business Web site seeking answers only to come away empty-handed and frustrated. At InQuira, we feel your pain.

Mike Murphy

I dedicate this book to the very special individuals that made a difference by inspiring my life long quest for knowledge. My father, William, who always explained to me the scientific "why" and the "how" of everything around me as I grew up. My scoutmaster, Don Rouse, who encouraged me to complete all the work to become an Eagle Scout. My favorite high school teacher, Gerald Walker, who assisted me in obtaining a scholarship to the University of Notre Dame. My mentor at Notre Dame, Professor Art Quigley, who guided me through the steps of gaining access to the graduate program at Harvard University to pursue and complete my Doctorate. My doctoral thesis advisor, Professor Edward Radford, who helped me create the "vision" of the original research required to complete my degree in record time. My very special and most loyal friend, Professor Richard Feinberg, who gave me the opportunity to create the Center for Customer-Driven Quality at Purdue University that changed the course of my career in a multitude of ways. To each of these great men, I owe a special thanks for "being there" for me at a mission-critical moment in my life. Thank you....

Dr. Jon Anton

Table of Contents

List of Figures

We wish to thank Patrick O'Neal, the CEO and President, of the Sento Corporation for his insightful contributions to Chapter 6. Pat has led his company to becoming a leader in seamless channel integration strategies that allow customers to have choices at each juncture of their search for information from companies.

We wish to thank Bob Chatham of Forrester Research for taking the time to write the foreword for our book.

We wish to thank both Michael Spinelli and David Daniels of Jupiter Media for their contributions to Chapter 15. We also wish to thank David Daniels for writing a foreword to this book.

We wish to thank Cory Gideon Gunderson, our Technical Writer, and Anita Rockwell, our Content Editor, for their major individual efforts to make this book into a true compendium about Web-based customer experience management.

And finally, we wish to thank our production team, including Debi Cloud, Susan Hampton, and Gail Carver, for their very professional work in taking our numerous drafts of the manuscript, and transforming its many words, graphs, and tables into an attractive and readable book.

By

Bob Chatham
Forrester Research

We've spent the last 50 years teaching customers that good service means a business answers the phone on the first ring. So it's no wonder that only one-third of online self-service efforts pay off—there are a lot of old habits to break.

Most firms don't have the perseverance to prove to customers that self-service can actually mean better service. Their efforts stumble along with a poor understanding of customers' service preferences, bad experience designs, and hazy ROI measures. That's why nearly 20% of online service initiatives end up *increasing* call traffic to customer service agents—far from the original goal of cutting service costs.

For firms to tap the Internet's benefits they have to first enable customers to meet their goals, whatever they are: research their next car, book travel, get service, or just have fun. Forrester calls this bargain with customers *right-channeling*—providing a compelling customer experience that meets both customer—and company—goals.

To give customers the right service, at the right time, in the right channel, executives must leverage the Internet's blend of Web self-service, chat, e-mail, and access to agents. This book delivers insight into all of these options, and—most importantly—into the critical organizational and operational best practices that will help companies manage the transition to the Internet as a way to deliver not just low-cost, but great customer service.

By

David Daniels
Senior Analyst
Jupiter Research

Not since the introduction of call routing systems and touch-tone based self-service systems in the early 1970s have we seen such a frenzy to drive customers into self-service transactions. By its very nature, the Internet is a self-service application, and has provided a tremendous set of new tools. It is spurring on a corporate renaissance of sorts, as we all look to fresh approaches to improve upon old ideas.

The Internet revolution is in full swing, with its adoption amongst consumers rivaling that of cable television. In 2004, Jupiter Research forecasts that 81% of U.S. households will have personal computers and that 90% of them will have Internet access. No other consumer technology medium has been available to and used by so many individuals in such a short period of time. Yet as consumers flock to the Internet, it is accelerating the growth of customer service contacts, which online will total more than 5.3 billion in 2008.

Massive Internet adoption, rising service requests and the maturation of natural language processing technology is creating the perfect storm for online self-service. Early adopters of self-service search such as Bank of America and BEA are realizing improvements in customer satisfaction and contact center efficiency, because they are not solely focused on contact deflection, but rather on the customer's experience. Customer Experience Management surpasses the conventional notion of IVR (interactive voice response) self-service, in that the natural language query provides the ability to dictate the customer's self-service experience—whether that is returning content, a chat session or propelling the customer into a task such as a loan application.

The opportunity to satisfy customers anytime by allowing them to search for their own service solutions is compelling, but far more complex than presenting a simple search box on a site and returning a laundry of list of possible results. Perfecting Customer Experience

Management necessitates taking a grounded approach to the fancy wizardry that the Internet affords us and begins with classic business practices, such as identifying objectives, assessing corporate readiness and measurement.

In "Managing Web-Based Customer Experiences," Jon Anton and Mike Murphy offer a compelling and insightful view of the underlying principles and tactics necessary to limit self-service risks and exploit its opportunities. Their pragmatic advice, data points and case studies provide excellent guidance in navigating the road to self-service success. You will surely learn from this text and I hope you enjoy it as much as I did.

As can be seen from figure 1.1, customer contacts are forecasted to reach the 30 billion mark by 2005 and are divided mostly across the telephone, e-mail, chat, and Web site channels.

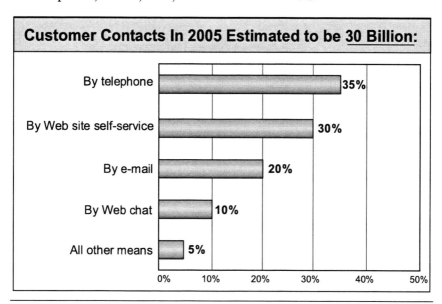

Figure 1.1. Channel usage by 2005

The importance of the data in this figure is that it shows how Americans demand contact with companies from whom they buy products—and that contact is before, during, and after the sale. The most popular of these channels is also the most expensive channel, the live telephone contact. The most important purpose of this book is to determine if self-service on the Web site can, in time, deflect many of the less valuable contacts between customers and companies.

It is clear to us that every CEO wants all of the following:

1. to decrease costs (be more efficient)
2. to increase customer-sat (to be more effective)
3. to increase revenues (to add to the bottom line)
4. to increase wallet share (to make customers more loyal)

1

5. to increase market share (to acquire more customer knowledge)

The value of this book lies not only in its power to help you increase customer satisfaction through the implementation of Web self-service, but also to achieve all five of the CEO's most often stated "demands," as outlined on the previous page. As the illustration below points out, the value of this book can also be calculated in terms of calls deflected from your call center, increased customer retention, and ultimately in a healthy return on your investment.

ROI Factors: Customer Self-Service

- **Call Deflection**

    (# of online visitors) *

    (% of Searchers) *

    (% Improvement Over Search Accuracy) *

    (% Unsuccessful Searchers who Call in) *

    (Avg. Cost per Call)

    +

    (# of online prospects)

    (% of non-Searchers)

    (% Improvement Over Browsing Accuracy) *

    (% non-Searchers who switch to InQuira)

    (% Unsuccessful non-Searchers who Call in) *

    (Avg. Cost per Call)

- **Customer Retention**

    (# of online visitors) *

    (% of Searchers) *

    (% Improvement Over Search Accuracy) *

    (% Unsuccessful Searchers NOT to Call in) *

    (Avg. Life Time Customer Value) *

    (% Loss due to Customer Dissatisfaction)

    +

    (# of online prospects)

    (% of non-Searchers)

    (% Improvement Over Browsing Accuracy) *

    (% non-Searchers who switch to InQuira)

    (% Unsuccessful Searchers NOT to Call in) *

    (Avg. Life Time Customer Value) *

    (% Loss due to Customer Dissatisfaction)

Figure 1.2. ROI factors

The time to grow your call center into a multi-channel customer contact center is now. As figure 1.3 shows, your organization has a lot at stake. Our research shows that e-Business will grow from $72 billion to $217 billion over the next five years. Driving this revenue growth is the fact that more than 45 million consumers will be cross channel shoppers by 2005. It is also important to note that 42 percent of U.S. Web-buying consumers made their most recent purchase because of a previous good experience with the retailer.

Customers are taking a large part in driving the increased need for Web self-service. A full 60 percent of financial services customers were willing to give up human assistance if appropriately motivated. And it is in your best interest to motivate as many of your customers to make this move as possible. Consider that, on average, it costs $15 to service a customer using a live customer service rep versus just seven cents to service their needs via the Web. Perhaps this explains why most companies are experiencing a 50 percent annual growth rate in the number of Web pages they host.

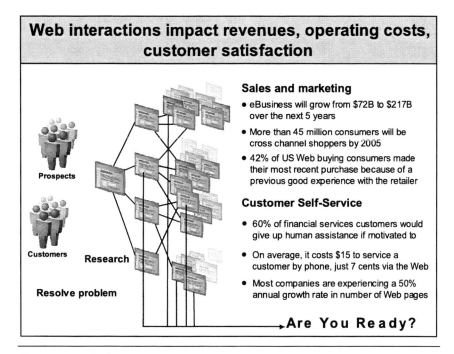

Figure 1.3. Web interactions impact revenues, operating costs, customer satisfaction

The ability to meet and surpass customer expectations is the primary determiner of an organization's long term viability. In other words, "if your customers ain't happy, then nobody's happy."

But, as anyone who's ever been charged with customer happiness knows, this goal is easier said than done. Customers are becoming more sophisticated, they're becoming more starved for time, and they're becoming more aware of the options they have to take their business elsewhere.

Savvy business leaders are learning that they can't stake their futures on satisfied customers. A 1994 study in the *Harvard Business*

Review examined this topic. The study referenced the 1-5 rating system used in many organizations to measure customer satisfaction levels (five represents the highest level of customer satisfaction). The authors of this study challenged organizations that were content with a score of 3.5 to 4.5, which indicates that customers are "satisfied" with their consumer experience. A "satisfied customer," the authors caution, should not be mistaken for a loyal customer. They report that a score from 3.5 to 4.5 reveals that customers are satisfied but **indifferent**. A score of 4.6 or above, on the other hand, indicates a **loyal** customer (Nunley, 2002). In our research, only "top-box" scores, i.e. 5 out of 5, indicate experiences that insure customer loyalty.

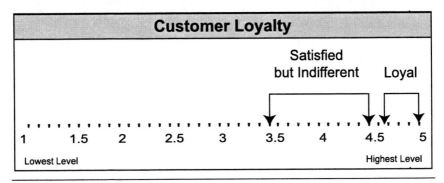

Figure 1.4. Customer loyalty

Add to this reality the fact that as markets reach higher and higher levels of saturation new customers become harder to find. This phenomenon forces companies to focus more and more on their existing customer relationships. Simultaneously, in almost every market, products have reached a high level of parity; the customer can hardly tell one product from another in terms of product features, quality, and/or price. In fact, in today's business world, having products that are of impeccable quality with robust features at very reasonable prices are the "table stakes" of being in business.

With competition stiffer than ever before, and markets crowded with competing products, many companies have begun initiatives to focus on customer experience management as the one remaining product differentiator. Typically, customer experience improvements come from the improvement and reengineering of three areas, namely the people, the process(es), and the technology of customer service.

For many companies, the customer experience focus has been on better customer service through improved recruiting, screening, and training. Perhaps, though, the best customer service of all is not achieved by adding more or better front line employees. We propose that the best way to create loyal customers is to design more effective and more efficient ways to allow customers to help themselves. We propose self-service and assisted-service.

Yesterday's customers may have resigned themselves to the limitations of conducting their business via the telephone. The long wait times, the restricted business hours, dealing with the customer service representative (CSR) just fresh out of training may once have been accepted as the norm, but is definitely not true anymore.

Today's customers are a different breed. As technology has advanced, so have customer expectations. Today's customers expect quick, top quality, personalized service, at a time that's convenient for them. These increasingly common expectations are one driver of the authors' estimate that by 2005, over 70% of all business interactions would be conducted over the Internet (eGain, 2001). Managing this new customer experience on the Web is even more of a challenge as depicted in figure 1.5.

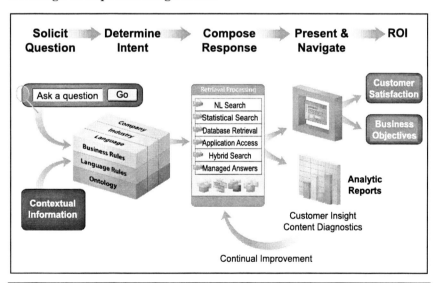

Figure 1.5. Creating an effective experience for customers and businesses

If you have any doubts as to the prevalence of electronic interaction and self-service opportunities, consider the self-service experiences one of the authors had on a recent trip:

- bought my United e-ticket on the Web
- reserved a specific hotel room on the Web
- at the airport, used United kiosk to get boarding pass
- used the Hertz "never get lost" in-car navigation system to find my hotel
- checked myself in with the lobby kiosk
- bought and sent my wife flowers on a Web site
- on the way home, stopped to pump my own gas
- at the nearby grocery store, checked myself out with a carton of milk
- did I like serving myself—I loved it!!!

Yet, the demand for phone-based service continues to rise. And the call to cut costs is as clear as ever. So what's a leader to do? Those leaders on the cutting edge of customer satisfaction have embraced the new reality: the need for a business model that supplements the traditional call center with other channels of interaction. The integration of self-service and assisted-service.

Self-service, quite simply, can be defined as "any solution that allows a (internal or external) customer to achieve his or her objective without the help of another person." Ideally, assisted self-service will be seamless. Assisted self-service is "any solution that allows a customer who has first tried self-service to seamlessly transition to a live agent without the loss of information already provided by the customer."

When done well, this blended business model increases an organization's opportunity to create loyal customers. It puts the customer in control of how, when, and from where they contact you. The point is to create consistent and seamless interactions, no matter which avenue of communication the customer chooses.

The beauty of consistent and seamless interactions is that not only is customer satisfaction increased, but shareholder satisfaction is, too. According to the American Customer Satisfaction Index Web site, "...firms with the top 50% of ACSI scores generated an average of $24 billion in shareholder wealth while firms with the bottom 50% of scores only created $14 billion." (Thompson, 2002)

A recent CRM Guru study revealed that one-third of companies are using some form of e-Service. It said most are in-house efforts that are cobbled together with static HTML pages, manually maintained FAQs, and e-mail service powered by CSRs. This current-state-of-the-contact-center picture likely explains why a recent benchmarking study found that 50% of all attempts by customers to find online service ended up in a call to the contact center (Thompson, 2002).

There is clearly a difference between offering Web self-service and delivering *effective* Web self-service. Figure 1.6 shows what it takes to deliver the latter. Effective Web self-service allows customers the ability to research, respond with answers, resolve their issues, conduct transactions, and escalate issues as necessary. It empowers businesses to acquire customers, sell products, cross-sell, up-sell, manage escalations effectively, and, ultimately, to reduce costs.

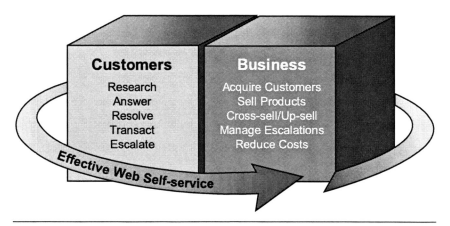

Figure 1.6. Web self-service must meet customer and business needs

In today's global economy, only a strategic business approach to meeting customer expectations will be effective. That's what this book is about. To arm you with the information you need to transform your call center into an effective contact center. To provide you with the knowledge you need to create not just satisfied customers, but loyal ones. And to help you realize a healthy return on your investment (ROI).

Figure 1.7 shows the actual annual savings one Fortune 500 bank realized when it implemented an effective Web self-service program. It should be noted that the savings of over three and a half million reflect 25 percent of this organization's total calls deflected to Web self-service. As you will read later, a commitment to continuous improvement can mean even greater savings.

For a Fortune 500 Retail Bank, a **25% increase in calls deflected** resulted in **$3.62M** per year in total cost savings.

Assumptions:
- Cost per call = $5
- 4.5% of visitors using InQuira
- Accuracy improvement in providing right information of 50%

For a large Mutual Fund company, a **1% improvement in conversion rate** (new customer acquisition) resulted in **$2.17M** per year in additional revenue.

Assumptions:
- Customer Life Time Value = $5,000
- 4.5% of prospects using InQuira
- Accuracy improvement in providing right information of 50%

Figure 1.7. Self-service pays off

While business relationships have always been based on a series of interactions, the nature of those interactions has changed significantly over the years. Face-to-face relationships are not as common as they used to be. Today's companies typically manage a larger group of customers with fewer customer-facing employees. It is increasingly rare to find a CSR who works with the same customer over the relationship's lifecycle. While small business owners may still be able to maintain effective customer relationships manually, businesses that compete in the global economy cannot.

This change in landscape has necessitated a wider variation in the types of channels businesses offer their customers. Telephones, e-mail, chat, kiosk, and Web offerings have become common. Each of these channels has it owns benefits and challenges. Figure 2.1 shows the four critical business objectives needed to deliver a quality online customer experience.

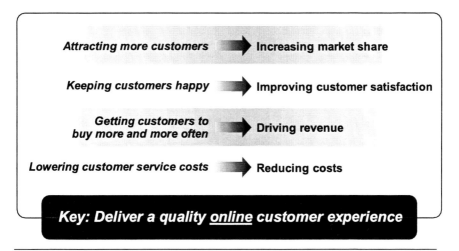

Figure 2.1. Four critical business objectives

Telephone

A recent study by Purdue University showed that the telephone is still the main channel for customer interaction. It represents 85% of all contacts in 2000. This same study predicted that by 2005, the telephone will account for only 45% of all contacts (eGain, 2002).

The following two figures illustrate how things are predicted to change by 2005. The first graph, *Customer Contacts in 2000,* clearly shows that the vast majority of contacts came into calls centers via the telephone. Together, e-mail and Web site contacts only accounted for five percent of contacts.

Contrast that to what we predict will happen to the nature of customer contacts between now and 2005. Trends are showing that within a few years only 45 percent of all customer contacts will be via the telephone. The combination of Web site contacts and e-mail contacts will have risen to 45 percent.

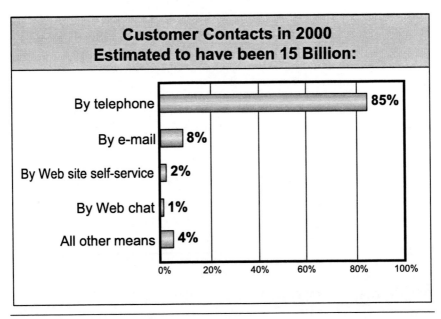

Figure 2.2. Customer contacts in 2000 estimated to have been 15 billion

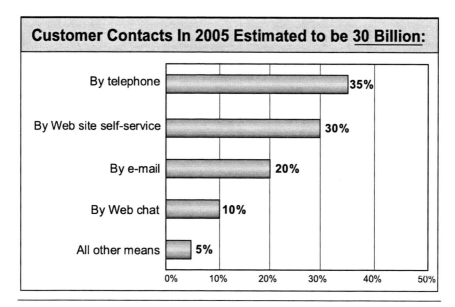

Figure 2.3. Customer contacts in 2005 estimated to be 30 billion

For visual customers especially, phone interaction has its limitations. Many customers want to see a product before they buy it. Even in customer service, a picture is often worth a thousand words.

No doubt, customers' frustration with the telephone service they've received over the years is partly responsible for this projected decrease. Customers are tired of restricted call center hours, tired of being kept on hold, and tired of being bounced around. They're tired of CSRs who are not always as knowledgeable as they should be, or as consistently polite as they're expected to be.

While customer demand is driving the need for alternative channels of communication, it is not the only catalyst. With labor representing 60 to 75 percent of the cost of running a contact center, leaders have great incentive to offer alternate channels of communication to their customers. A study of trends over the past half century reveals that employees now cost substantially more than they did 50 years ago. Yet, organizations are getting substantially less in terms of results from their front line people (Anton, James, Small, 1996). Add to this "people issue" the fact that contact centers will face a labor shortage as the baby boomers retire in a few years.

Factor into this scenario the increasingly complex information that CSRs have to learn, and you're looking at pretty steep labor costs. Then look beyond employees' initial training, and consider recurrent training costs: Training materials, trainer costs, and service rep time away from the phone. It should come as no surprise that a single customer telephone call with a live CSR can run as high as $50. The practical implication of this high price tag is that organizations typically end up restricting hours of operation and placing fewer than needed agents to handle call volumes (Kaneshige, 2002).

Figure 2.4. Today's agents are more complex and more expensive

Figure 2.5 shows a 2001 Forrester Research finding that illustrates the difference in organizational cost between Web self-service, e-mail, and phone customer contacts. While costs will vary among industries, the message is clear. While the need for live telephone CSRs will remain for the foreseeable future, the more contacts we deflect from them, the more we save.

Our own studies of Web-based chat as a very viable, yet barely used live channel, indicates that the typical chat session costs on average $2.50, or between 1/3 to 1/4 the cost of a phone call.

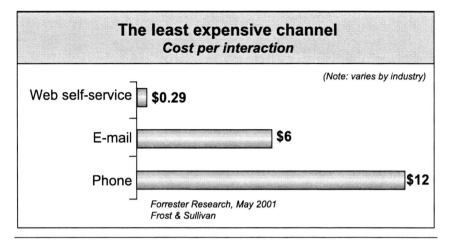

Figure 2.5. The current average cost per access channel

E-mail

Many organizations today are deluged with customer-generated e-mail. In today's economy, millions use this mode of correspondence daily. E-mail is currently the single most often used Internet activity. Forrester Research predicts that the current volume will continue to rise sharply and steadily. While e-mail currently supplements telephone-based service in many contact centers, others are moving towards making e-mail their primary channel for customer service (eGain, 2001).

E-mail is often more convenient for customers to use than the telephone. It is also costs organizations considerably less to respond to e-mails than it does to respond to a phone call. Yet, customer satisfaction with this means of communicating is unnecessarily low.

Studies reveal a consistent list of customer complaints regarding e-mail:

- Customers never received a response to their e-mail or their response was inexplicably delayed. One study revealed that two out of five e-mails go unanswered.

- The response customers received contained too little or incorrect information.

- The customers received poorly written replies.

When customers are dissatisfied with a company's reply to their e-mail, they will frequently end up placing a call to that company's contact center. The customers' dissatisfaction is fueled when service reps have no history of their e-mail or e-mails, and the customers have to repeat their issue or inquiry.

There is currently a significant gap between the current e-mail service performance and customer expectations. This discrepancy can be attributed to two things. First, some companies try to get by using personal e-mail systems such as Lotus Notes or Microsoft Outlook for their customer service needs. Unfortunately, customer e-mails can quickly overtax most personal e-mail systems. The Gartner Group recommends that organizations that receive 50 or more e-mails a day consider an e-mail response management system (eGain, 2001).

Secondly, some contact center leaders naively implement their contact centers' phone processes in their e-mail environment without realizing the significant differences between the two. An example is that a surge in phone calls to a contact center can lead to abandoned calls whereas a surge in e-mails over the holidays will not go away. The e-mails will be on perpetual "hold" until they're answered. The two scenarios, neither desirable, will require different staffing strategies.

The mishandling of customer e-mail can be costly to an organization. One study showed that 64 percent of retail customers would likely stop doing business with a company that didn't respond to their e-mail within what they considered to be an acceptable time frame (eGain, 2001).

Web Chat

Web chat-based help provides customers live (real-time) personal assistance when they're on an organization's Web site. The customer types in questions, and the CSR responds with a typed reply. This interchange goes back and forth until, ideally, the customer's issue is resolved and/or his order is placed.

Web chat is also a helpful communication avenue for the customer who needs help in completing an online form. A CSR can send a text message to the customer that guides the customer through the transaction. A helpful service rep can also use Web chat to answer customers' questions during their online shopping experience. The hope is that the representative can prevent an abandoned shopping cart.

While some contact leaders place Web chat in the same category as e-mail, it cannot be assumed that a CSR who is proficient at answering e-mails is fully qualified to respond to customers' Web chat. Service reps who communicate via Web chat must be tuned into the fact that customers don't like to feel ignored. This reality requires service reps to display a committed, consistent sense of urgency in replying to customer inquiries. Live text interactions also require ideas be communicated more concisely than e-mail correspondence necessitates. Management also must ensure that there are ample CSRs to get the job done with quality.

The blessing and curse of text-Web chat interactions are that they, like e-mails, are recorded in writing. When interactions are well handled by an organization's CSRs, this documentation can be very helpful. A paper trail of a poor service scenario would not always be considered a blessing to contact center leadership, especially if legal issues arise.

Here are two company's perspectives on Web chat:

Lands' End has offered service through the use of text messaging since 1999. Angie Rundle, Lands' End supervisor of Internet sales, says "the value to the customer is having help readily available to them." Customers don't have to "log off their PC and call." This is helpful considering that most homes still don't have two phone lines (Lieber, 2003).

The contact center director at gift Web site Red Envelope, Susan Helscher, notes that customers tend to use Web chat when "they really are in need of an urgent or quick response. We see a spike at holiday time, not just because of volume but because of that urgency." (Lieber, 2003)

While Web chat options have benefited some organizations, we expect a 10-to-1 ratio of e-mail messages to live text messages as contact centers evolve. Surprisingly, considering how popular instant messaging is today, customers have not demonstrated a preference for Web chat options.

While many Gen X and Y members have embraced instant messaging and would likely appreciate Web chat as a service option, baby boomers are not showing their receptiveness to Web chat.

A typical CSR response to a customer inquiry or complaint during a Web chat sessions costs an organization at least the same amount as does a live service rep responding to a telephone call. This has driven many organizations to have their CSRs handle multiple Web chat conversations simultaneously.

The risk these organizations take is that they may be biting off more than their CSRs can chew. If customer service slips because your representatives are too overwhelmed to meet and exceed customer expectations, you may end up losing revenue. And, worse, you may end up losing customers. A case of penny wise being pound foolish!

Kiosk

Some organizations are using self-service kiosks to bridge their product or service to the customer. Kiosks abound in airports, movie theaters, hotel lobbies, banks, grocery stores, and numerous other places. One industry analyst predicted that by 2006, consumers would buy $6.5 billion dollars worth of products and services via kiosks (Netkey, Inc., 2002).

Borders Books offers a vivid example of the power kiosks have to generate sales. Through the company's *Title Sleuth* kiosk, users typically purchase 20 percent more product than do other customers. In 2001, Staples, the office supply chain, identified $200 million dollars in revenue that were attributed to its in-store kiosks. And Kodak's *Picture Maker Kiosk* reportedly pays for itself in less than six months (Netkey, Inc., 2002).

You might be surprised by the wide range of uses for kiosks. The Superior Court of Arizona recently instituted a program called *Quick Court*. This program lets married couples file for divorce using computerized kiosks. This does away with the need for lawyers and, in some cases, court proceedings (Anton, James, and Small, 1996).

Yet, kiosks, like all technology, have their limitations. For starters, not all products and services can be sold through kiosks. Just picture a hospital or health insurer trying to sell their products and services through this channel. And then there is the issue of maintaining the kiosk's hardware and software in multiple, remote locations. Once a kiosk is put into a retail location, its owner has given up a degree of control over the consumer experience.

Internet—Web

The Web (a.k.a. the Internet) has revolutionized the way customers and companies interact. Company information is put on the Web so customers can search a database and find answers for themselves. Often this service eliminates the need for customers to call a company's contact center.

Customers today can expect to check their bank balances, bid on and purchase products, request library books, and even self-diagnose their ailments online. The life changing power of the Web can be appreciated by the success of companies like Amazon.com and eBay. Did our grandparents ever imagine the day they could purchase products without having to visit a brick and mortar store or place a phone order?

A recent study performed by BenchmarkPortal showed just how much the Web has made its way into our lives. Consider the following statistics.

- 67 million people use the Web daily
- 58% shop for a car on the Web before going to the dealer
- 89% shop on the Web before deciding where to go on vacation
- 72% shop airline tickets on the Web

Figure 2.6. The overwhelming acceptance of the Web

When a Web strategy is implemented well, it typically results in significant improvements to customer service as well as significant organizational savings.

Yet, the Web continues to be a challenge for many organizations. Most companies are still searching for the way to best leverage the Web's full power and promise.

Unfortunately, today's Web service is still considered by many to be in its infancy. A report by InQuira sums up the current state of Web service and contact center affairs:

It's a major problem, and every enterprise knows about it.

Corporate Web sites are not making customers happy. Search engines are limited and rudimentary. Service, support and even sales assistance is inconsistent, slow, and frequently ineffective. It's no wonder that customer loyalty lasts about as long as it takes to get to the next competitor's Web site.

For end users, a poorly functioning Web site can mean getting locked into a loop of incompetence. The user, looking for an answer to a question, tries browsing the site. That doesn't work. The next step, trying the search engine, wastes even more time, as the user sifts through inadequate results. The user then picks up the phone, runs through menus, waits in a queue, and finally gets to a live CSR—who doesn't have the answer. Now the CSR tries to find it, searching the company Intranet, and typically invoking the same search engine the user started with.

For the enterprise, the Web site brings a different kind of pain. Trying to provide good service and hold down costs at the same time, the enterprise often can do neither. Customers are leaving because of bad service, and any attempts to fix the problem are driving site costs into the stratosphere (InQuira White Paper, The Customer-to-Enterprise Connection: Fundamental Problems, Rudimentary Solutions).

Figure 2.7 depicts just why so many current Web self-service experiences fail. Existing customers or potential customers go to a site to: ask a question, make a purchase, research an issue, resolve a problem, or to escalate an issue. Instead of walking away from the customer contact with a product or solution, many get mired in a site that has content buried so deeply within it that the customer gives up before they've found it. Other times a solution doesn't even exist on the site or the search tool isn't effective enough to connect the proper solution to the customer query. Needless to say, few organizations can afford to miss so many opportunities to make a sale or to increase customer loyalty.

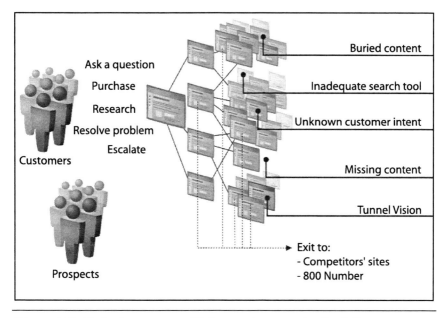

Figure 2.7. Today's corporate Web experience typically fails

A November 2002 AMR Research survey showed that more than 70 percent of those surveyed said that they planned to invest in e-mail management or contact center tools by the end of 2004. We are encouraged that so many organizations recognize their need to better meet customer needs. We propose, however, that before you begin to purchase and implement contact center solutions you consider our observations that Americans have a natural tendency toward being "do-it-yourself individualists." (Kaneshige, 2002)

While deciding on how you will spend your organization's hard won money to create loyal customers, consider designing more effective and more efficient ways to allow customers to help themselves—via Web self-service. We believe that the best service is self-service because:

1. it is often substantially less expensive
2. it is often faster, more consistent, and more reliable
3. it is often available at all hours of the day and night

Technology and process improvements that foster customer self-service almost always result in large gains in customer satisfaction and substantial decreases in process costs. This combination, in turn, typically results in a high return on investments. Moving to self-service perfectly fits the goal and definition of modern reengineering initiatives. Reengineering is defined as the fundamental re-thinking and radical re-design of a company's service process to achieve measured performance improvements in cost, quality, service, and speed.

The following chapters will help you better understand how a well planned and effectively implemented self-service initiative will help you achieve and maintain your company's competitive advantage in a hypercompetitive market. To do this, we will look at all angles of this topic from the pitfalls of customer self-service to the design and implementation of a successful self-service strategy—a strategy that can delight customers and keep them loyal to you.

CHAPTER 3: CALL CENTER CHANNEL USERS

Recently, the authors conducted research, sponsored by Kelly Services, to determine the demographics of customers who use the call center channel. The purpose of this research was to survey a statistical sample of the American population to determine:

1. why they called
2. what companies they called
3. how happy they were with the call handling
4. the demographics and psychographics of the callers

Key Demographics of Americans that Contact Company Call Centers

A sampling of the demographics of Americans that contact call centers are as follows:

- the majority are between 26 and 55 years old
- more than 50 percent have at least a four-year college degree
- the average income is more than $50,000 per year

The results of this study confirmed that those that contact companies through the call center channel definitely are Web-enabled and can be convinced to try self-service on the Web, if properly positioned. The complete study can be downloaded from our Web site at <www.BenchmarkPortal.com>. The following pages show some of the key findings from this research engagement.

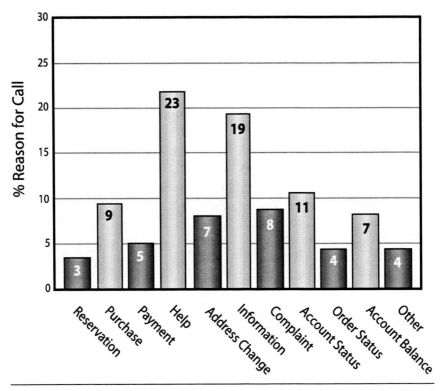

Figure 3.1. Why do Americans call companies?

Question:	What was the reason for your last call to a company?
Finding:	This figure shows the various reasons that the participants called a call center, and the frequency in percent of how the participants responded. As you can see, "request for help with a product or service" was the most popular reason for the call at 23 percent of the total, with "request for information" a close second at 19 percent of the total call reasons.
Interpretation:	Accessibility to information and assistance through the telephone has become a "feature" expected by American consumers of every product and service. The call center can be an effective channel to deliver this important feature.

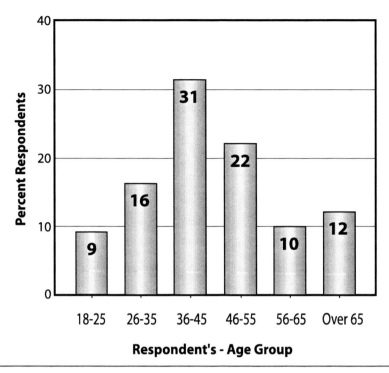

Figure 3.2. What is the age distribution of American callers?

Question: Which age group do you belong to?

Finding: In this figure we see the frequency of various age groupings in our research on who uses the telephone to contact companies. As was expected, the majority of the respondents were in the age range of 26 to 55 years old, with the peak group being between 36 and 45 years old.

Interpretation: This is an important finding for companies with a call center. The age range from 36 to 45 is certainly a group of Americans that companies want to attract and service properly, since this age group is the most active in contacting companies for assistance and for information.

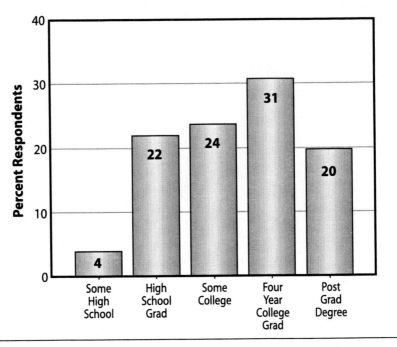

Figure 3.3. What is the education level of American callers?

Question: What is your level of education?

Finding: This figure shows there is an even spread between high school graduates and college-educated respondents. Seventy-five percent of the respondents have at least some college education, and 51 percent of the respondents have four or more years of college education.

Interpretation: In our opinion, the demographics and psychographics of the population that most companies target their products to is the same group that is most likely to call the toll-free number for assistance and/or for information. This is an important finding that should motivate companies to make sure their call center is all that it can be in delivering superb quality service to this kind of customer.

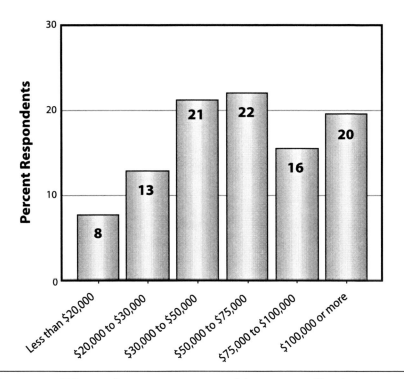

Figure 3.4. What is the average income of American callers?

Question: Please share with us your annual income.

Finding: This figure shows the distribution of annual household income for the respondents. Almost eighty percent are in the "$30,000+" per year bracket. Fifty-eight percent are in the "$50,000+" per year bracket.

Interpretation: The importance of this finding for companies is to emphasize that the typical American calling a contact center has substantial annual income and buying power and future purchasing influence.

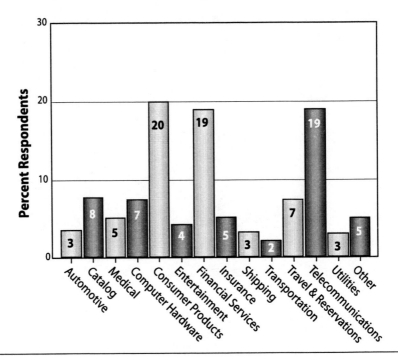

Figure 3.5. What industries do Americans call most?

Question:	From the following list, please indicate the industry of the company you last called for customer service.
Finding:	The participant was asked which industry category the company he/she called fell into. The breakdown of these categories is displayed in the figure above.
Interpretation:	As we expected, consumer products, financial services, and telecommunications represent the majority of companies called in this study.

CHAPTER 4: INTRODUCTION TO CUSTOMER SELF-SERVICE

A Definition

While many definitions of self-service likely exist, we define it as "any solution that allows an internal or external customer to achieve his or her objective without the help of another person." Notice that this definition goes horizontally across your company and cuts through all your internal departments and "silos." It includes everything from sales, order placement, order tracking, order fulfillment, installation, product utilization, etc.

This book covers all products from tangible (i.e. food, cars, and clothing) to intangible service products (i.e. an airline seat, hotel room, delivery service). The critical mission of any customer service strategy is to manage the customer experiences such that the sum total of the customer's experiences are so fantastic that the customer's loyalty is ensured. Another part of that mission is for the customer to consider you unquestionably as the "preferred supplier," or company of choice. This in itself can be a very important advantage to using well-designed and tested self-service technology in that it can deliver consistent service any time of the day or night.

While phone self-service, like all technology, has its own strengths and limitations, this book is focused primarily on Web self-service.

The Driving Forces

In 1999, the Call Center Learning Center did a benchmarking study on call center best practices (Hiatt, 2002). The center received results from 102 call centers. In 2001, the center received results on the same topic from more than 270 organizations. According to the center, "The core principles have proven to be lasting concepts for creating a contact center that delivers excellent customer service at the lowest possible cost." Interestingly, the top three (out of eight) *principles driving world-class call center design* all point to the need for companies to offer self-service. These include:

Principle 1: Give customers choice

Customers expect to choose how they interact with you. Your service must be by their standards and by the media of their choice. Telephone service cannot be the only media for customer service.

Principle 2: Provide access anytime, and anywhere

Access to services will be every hour of every day, from wherever the customer chooses.

Principle 3: Enable customers to help themselves

Customers will have access to information and can choose self-service or agent-assisted-service. Many customers will prefer to find information or initiate transactions on their own (Hiatt, 2002).

It is also interesting to note how the Call Center Learning Center benchmarking studies compared in regard to process and technology from 1999 to 2001. According to the center, there was a shift in priorities from 1999 to 2001 that showed "the increased focus on multi-media contact handling as a core competency for the call center."

In the study's summary, writer Jeff Hiatt warns that, "Incremental improvements will not be adequate to keep pace with growing customer demands for service that is anytime and anywhere. The need to re-design or reengineer the basic business processes around customer service will be an imperative for call center managers who are planning ahead for the next generation." (Hiatt, 2002)

If you think the customer's reasons for wanting self-service are compelling, consider an organization's reasons. According to Forrester Research, Web self-service is the most cost effective way to provide a customer full service. Forrester estimates that a customer's call to a live agent costs a company about $33. An e-mail is estimated to cost a company $10. And self-service, estimates Forrester, costs about $1 per inquiry (Robinson, 2002).

Consider now the typical reasons a customer places a call to a company. Our research, as illustrated in the next graph, shows that 65 percent of customers have a question that needs to be answered. Approximately 25 percent need to have something done; they need to place an order, change their address, etc. About 15 percent need something fixed; this can include anything from needing a watch repaired to having an intangible problem solved like straightening out a health care billing problem. About five percent call with a complaint (Anton, 2002).

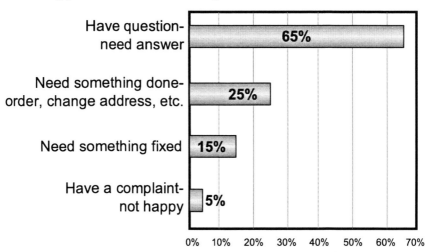

Figure 4.1. Typical reasons why customers call

Figure 4.2 shows what Web self-service can do. We propose that a large share of customers who have a question can find the answers they need via Web self-service. Most who need something done can, too. A third of those who need something fixed should be able to find resolution via self-service. We do not recommend that self-service as an appropriate communication avenue for those customers who want to lodge a complaint.

What Can Self-service Do?

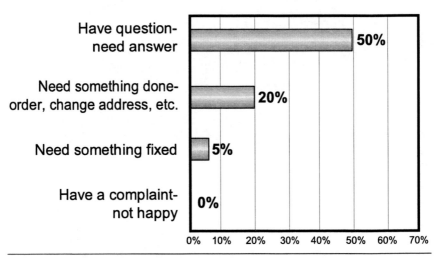

Figure 4.2. What can self-service do?

When you consider how many "low value" customer contacts (i.e. those that do not build customer loyalty or accomplish add-on sales) can be shifted to self-service, the potential savings are staggering.

If you're not currently offering Web self-service, your customers are probably wondering why. Is there something wrong with this company? Don't they know how to offer Web self-service? Are they technically challenged? Increasingly, customers are expecting Web self-service.

In a paper published by Gartner in 2002 titled *Time for a Change*, the author states that, "Fifteen to 40 percent of call volume will move to the Internet as consistent, less-complex problem types are solved via self-service at the Web site." Just imagine the potential for customer satisfaction and cost savings!

A recent Doculabs report stated that, "Based on results of over 3.7 million customer service requests made via the Web to over 200 companies in the first quarter of 2001, the cumulative total quarterly savings exceeding $100 million was realized through automated Web self-service. Based on these numbers, the companies in the index saved on average more than $500,000 per quarter and $165,000 per month." (Watson, 2002)

Cultural Differences

As we researched different cultures around the world, we noticed major differences regarding the individual cultures and the value they placed on Web-based self-service. Here is what we found:

1. Citizens of the majority of cultures were still not even marginally Internet enabled, therefore leaving them stranded in any self-service initiatives. This is however changing rapidly especially as the Asia-Pacific countries are coming online with a vengeance.

2. Americans are natural "do it yourselfers," and this shows with so many of the institutions that do well in North America, namely, the ATM, Home Depot, the salad bar, and the like. This makes Americans easy targets for self-service initiatives.

3. As long as there is "help" available, Americans will try anything, including self-service. It is interesting, that as we write this book, the airlines are all moving us carefully, yet decisively, to self-service ticketing and boarding pass printing through the kiosk. More about this later.

Over the past ten years, we have seen example after example of situations where customers much prefer to help themselves. They will choose self-service over waiting for a company representative for assistance. The following are a few of the better known examples in self-service.

The Salad Bar

Most adults can remember the days before the salad bar when we would sit and wait for a busy waiter. After waiting for what seemed like hours, the waiter would finally approach and take our order only to disappear again for endless minutes before bringing us a meager bowl of salad. Finally, astute restaurant owners realized that people are much happier when they are munching on something, and that making a salad can be both fun and entertaining. Combine that with the money saved in waiter time, and the salad bar revolution was born. Most of us love to make over-sized salads of a wide variety of fresh vegetables, and, amazingly enough, we are willing to pay for this privilege of doing it ourselves. We value the experience and get more for our money, and, of course, get the salad when we want it (Anton, James, Small, 1996).

Automated Teller Machine (ATM)

In the early 1980s, before deregulation, banks were very different. The inefficiencies were prevalent in almost all banking services. High on the list were the long lines at the bank teller counters, the odd banking hours (e.g., 10 a.m. to 3 p.m.) with an hour of additional closing at lunch, and, of course, no banking on Saturday or Sunday. The term "bankers' hours" was sort of a joke in those days because access to our own money and banking services were so limited. With a new focus on the customer, and with advances in technology, the old paradigm faded quickly.

We can learn a lot from the banks' experience with ATM's. What follows is an historical snapshot of self-service through the automatic teller machine.

1. In an effort to lower costs, the banking industry decided to move customers out of the lobby in order to:

   - allow the customer to help themselves with simple, low value transactions, like cash withdrawals, account balance information, and deposits

   - allow the customer access to their bank accounts 24 hours a day, by 7 days a week, by 365 a year

   - reduce head count and free up the best and more expensive tellers to conduct high-value transactions that induced the customer to use more of the banks products and services, and thereby ensured a higher degree of loyalty

2. This historic service initiative was not driven by the customer, in fact, the following was true at the time:

   - customers had a basic distrust of technology when it came to handling their money, even the "pass-book" saving instrument was still popular

   - customers were not nearly as computer literate as they are now

3. In fact, when the ATM first arrived on the bank walls, it was not accepted by the customer (i.e., people like you and me), mainly because:

   - it looked very bulky and complex

   - most customers were afraid of failing

4. What made the difference in acceptance was:

   - tellers were assigned to stand next to the ATM to assist customers in case of problems

   - the transactions proved to be simple and intuitive

   - most users marveled at the convenience, and they spread the word

5. The ATM proved to be a very cost effective self-service portal because:

   - it was available anywhere and at anytime, i.e., truly ubiquitous

   - standards evolved from bank to bank applications

   - low value transactions were handled by the customer without expensive personnel

6. Today customers do not use only the ATM because:

   - complex transactions need the "human touch"

   - people prefer to have choices when it comes to dealing with companies

The ATM became our personal teller any time of any day or night. The stampede to more and more self-service in banking leads to the prediction that brick and mortar banks are today's real dinosaurs. Now that most of us have our own PCs connected to the Web, the bank-without-walls is right around the corner. We don't really need tellers, do we (Anton, James, Small, 1996)? And the answer is, of course we need tellers, but not for many of the simple tasks. This is what we need to learn about the current customer service portals...let the customer do the simple, low value transactions themselves.

Automated Gas Pump

In the old days, the classic service station was notorious for its terrible service. The revolution was from full-service (if you could call it that) to self-service, which allowed us to pump our own gasoline. As customers, we were delighted as the savings were passed on to us and we could get in and out of the station much quicker on our own.

Even though we can now dispense our own gas at the pump, for a time we still had to endure the rain, sleet, and snow to do it. On top of that, we then had to make the trek to pay the human attendant for our gas purchase. Many of us longed for the old full-service days, until one day technology made it possible for us to use our credit card directly at the gas pump. We could complete the entire transaction by ourselves, which included getting a receipt for business travel. Nirvana! Self-service was a dream come true (Anton, James, Small, 1996)!

Automated Pharmacy Fulfillment

It wasn't that long ago that we had to stand in long lines at the pharmacy counter waiting to get our prescriptions filled. We'd wait to see the pharmacist or the pharmacy assistant; we'd wait some more for the order to be filled. If you didn't need sedatives going into the pharmacy, you might have needed them by the time you left.

Today, pharmacy chains offer customers the ability to place their refill order via an automated telephone system. Customers can designate their preference for pickup location and time with relative ease. When they make use of the pharmacy drive through feature, their experience is impressively pain free.

What these and other experiences teach us is that the best customer service may actually be one that is devoid of the sometimes cantankerous and occasionally abusive service employees. Let's face it; you can only do so much to improve the people element in customer service. And even the very best people aren't consistently great. Everyone has a bad day every now and then. Plus, really great front line people are hard to find and even harder to keep. In addition, if people don't have the inherited talent or service genes for front line work, the essential skills and attitudes are difficult to learn—even with the best coach or mentor.

The fundamental problem is providing the resources necessary to attract, train and retain excellent service agents. Since this requires a significant budget commitment, companies have historically tried to squeeze more and more cost out of the service component, which in many cases meant understaffing or lowering the hiring standards or training provided. By eliminating the easiest transactions (low value), the budget can be used to restore exceptional service levels for the more complex, value-added transactions.

Technology and process improvements that foster customer self-service almost always result in significant gains in customer satisfaction. They also typically result in substantial decreases in process cost. This means a high return on investments. And isn't that the bottom line?

CHAPTER 6: WHEN CUSTOMERS CHOOSE, COMPANIES WIN (AND SO DO THE CUSTOMERS)

Introduction

If you are like most people, you are probably asking questions like the following: What's a person to do? The whiz-bang isn't working and I need it to be working, *now!* Contact customer support, that's the answer. Should I pick up the phone or go to the Web site? Do I help myself or do I enlist the company's customer support pros?

Most people are beginning to embrace the self-service revolution. We give my bank money without ever stepping in the building. We see more ATMs than public restrooms these days. We now make flight reservations and check in online. Most of almost always use the pay-outside option when pumping gas, check ourselves out of hotels, and even buy movie tickets online. But while embracing the self-service revolution, there are times when we still want live help. When self-service is too slow or we're not in the mood, most want the option of live help. This does not necessarily mean that we want to speak with someone on the telephone. Sometimes that **is** what we want. However, sometimes we're not in the mood to carry on a conversation but we still want live help. There is e-mail but most companies treat those who communicate with them by e-mail as disreputable in-laws. What about chat? Our kids use it all the time but most of us are not completely comfortable with it!

Is There Any One Right Answer?

No, there are several right answers. And the right answer depends upon the circumstances and the mood of the customer at the time. So let the Customer have a Choice.

Why would a company dare to offer customers choices when we all know customers always choose the most expensive option? It's simple: lower cost and happier customers. When companies empower customers to transact how they want, when they want, we know from three years experience that the vast majority of customers will choose the lowest cost alternatives. That's what this chapter is all about, proving to you that informed customers choose the service options that are the least expensive to deliver.

The Case for Customer Choice

Not many years ago, nervous software companies shipped out 22 diskettes instead of one CD because the customer might not have a CD drive. They soon discovered that they were *punishing the many to serve the few*. The CD was better for the customer and cost the company less. Eventually, the CD was standard and latecomers were required to special-order the diskette packet; and customers applauded. What will make customers applaud in today's high-tech world? Getting an answer to their issue as quickly and as painlessly as possible. Here's how to do it.

Web Self Service

With 67 million American consumers on the Internet each day, we now represent the majority. With few exceptions, it is now possible for companies to give customers the tools that were historically only available to call-center agents and internal customer support people. In fact, it is not uncommon today for contact center agents to be using the same tools that the customer can access on the Web. During a phone call the agents are simply typing in what the customers could have done for themselves on the Web site had they only known. These tools fall into categories such as order placement, knowledge lookup, information tracking, customer profile, and as discussed earlier in this book, natural language information searches.

Savvy companies let customers reserve hotels, book airline tickets, order products, track shipments, and find for themselves answers provided in a well-managed and targeted knowledgebase accessed through natural language queries (natural language, as used here, is in contrast to using key word search). Really savvy companies reward these self-sufficient customers with lower costs and improved service.

Phone Self Service

While the phone cannot offer all of the benefits of the Web, voice-recognition technology (technology that can interpret the human voice) and interactive voice response (IVR) are taking this media to new heights. For example, banks are successfully providing customers with account information and airlines are providing flight arrival and departure details. And this can be done without using the keypad (good for those cell phone users who insist on driving while reading a map and talking on the phone). This self service media works in those situations where small amounts of data are gathered to deliver small amounts of data. For example, give me your telephone number and birth date and I will tell you the status of your order.

> NOTE: The key to successful self-service, regardless of how it is delivered, is to provide those options that are used frequently and successfully by customers. Too many companies try to deliver too much content and too many options, causing customers immediately to search for a phone number. The bank ATM illustrates this formula for success the best. Banks never intended for the ATM to replace the bank teller, only to handle cash withdrawal and balance transactions. And these they do quite frequently and successfully.

Why Internet Chat?

Internet chat has to be the most under-recognized and under-utilized communication method available to man. Some people believe that chat is a virtual 'chat room' where people with similar issues talk to each other. Not so! Internet chat for customer service is one-to-one, real-time communication over the Internet in a text environment. This option can be significantly more effective than phone or e-mail. Here is why.

- Chat allows customers to continue working on the Internet without cutting the connection to make a phone call. Even with broadband, talking on the phone while navigating the Web is a hassle.

- While using chat, customers can multi-task (deal with kids, eat a sandwich, navigate the Web, grab a credit card, or whatever). When on the phone, customers have the pressure of giving the agent full attention and blocking out all else.

- The chat agent can push URLs, co-browse Web pages, download files and (with permission) even take over control of the PC. This may seem a bit strange at first, but has great advantages in a technical support application.

- Since there is a transcript of the entire text conversation, if a customer is dissatisfied, the customer and the company avoid the 'he-said, she-said' scenario of the phone world.

- Chat agents can handle 2 to 3 customers simultaneously, without the customer being aware of this. Companies can use domestic and/or offshore agents, wherever Internet is available. For these reasons, chat is typically delivered at one-third the cost of a phone call. *(Note: While we have heard claims of chat agents handling as many as 5 or 6 chats at a time, we have found that 2 to 3 is both realistic and optimal.)*

- Managers have real-time visibility into the chat queues and individual interactions; this enables a high level of quality monitoring at any time from any place. Performance metrics such as customer satisfaction ratings, average handle time (AHT), and sales close rates are measured, analyzed and reported in an effort to drive higher standards. Performance metrics are measured at the center, team, and individual levels.

- First time resolution (FTR or FCR))rates are significantly higher than e-mail, and at least equal to those obtained over the phone.

Whereas phone agents live in the world of "let me tell you," *chat agents live in a world of "let me show you" or "let me do it for you."* Phone and e-mail cannot compare. The customer is better served and the company saves money. What is better than that?

E-mail Has its Place

We recently were Web shopping for an item and simply wanted to know if it was available in blue. We sent off a message, received an answer the next day, and was completely satisfied. There are times when we want help without the need or the hassle of waiting in a phone or chat queue. E-mail has its place, but is not equal to the synchronous communication options of Internet chat and phone.

It is not uncommon for a contact center to answer a customer's e-mail, only to discover that the customer had called in by phone in the interim... or sent several e-mails with the same issue. For this reason, contact centers introducing e-mail service often find that phone volume stays the same while overall costs have increased. *E-mail used for complicated or urgent issues leads to poor resolution rates, low customer satisfaction, and escalated costs.* Here is a basic set of guidelines for successful e-mail deployment:

- *Let customers understand that e-mail is for basic questions that don't require the agent to gather more information about the customer from the customer, i.e., no dialogue is required.* Also, be sure to provide a quick means of transitioning from e-mail to Internet chat or phone.

- Deliver e-mail through a Web form, avoiding narrative text altogether. If narrative text is allowed, limit the length to a fixed number of words or characters.

- *Do not use auto-response e-mail unless you have clearly set this expectation with the customer.* Auto-response will greatly degrade your reputation in Web-delivered service.

- Use e-mail primarily as a means of providing follow-up information (confirming an order, thanking the customer for contacting you, providing a link for tracking a shipment, and so on).

- *Set an expectation on turn-around time that you can meet or exceed.* Otherwise, customers will send multiple messages and may call you as well.

- Invest in e-mail technology that will allow you to manage queues and measure performance.

Reducing (Not Eliminating) Phone Volume

Phone service is undeniably the most expensive form of service. So why offer it at all? To start with, it may be the only option available to a customer at a given point in time, e.g., when the customer is traveling and/or otherwise does not have access to the Internet. Or Internet service could be down. Or the kids may be monopolizing the computer to chat with their friends (so called instant messaging, a.k.a. 'IM'ing). Or… since written communication (chat and e-mail) doesn't always provide the perfect forum for expressing emotion, customers may just want to speak with someone.

With that said, we submit to you that *customers generally do not prefer the phone*. In our experience (as shown in the case studies to follow), customers choose non-phone options at least 80%-90% of the time. Too often, companies position self-service, chat, and e-mail as ways of pushing the customer away. Here are some *tips for successfully diverting customers from the phone toward other options*:

- Create a self-service environment that parallels the ATM model. Specifically, deliver those features that are used often and will be used successfully in this environment. Don't try to replace live service with the 'everything-for-everyone' self-service engine. Think ATM!

- Provide customers with a simple transition to a live agent. Too many companies create a robust self-service engine and hide their phone number deep within the site.

- Give the customer enough information to make an informed choice as to what live option they should use (e.g., queue times, handle times, and maybe cost).

- Reward your customers for using your less expensive service options. For example, if your phone hours are Monday through Friday, 8am to 5pm, provide 24x7 Internet chat service. If wait times for the phone are typically 3 to 4 minutes, provide chat service within 1 minute.

- *Require customers to first visit your Web site before calling.* Eliminate inbound phone numbers altogether, and instead have the customer request a call back via the Web. The request is routed to a contact center that makes an outbound call. Or provide the customer with a PIN that they are required to enter into the IVR when calling. Customer rewards include no phone charges and more accurate routing to agents with the required skills to handle the customer's issue quickly.

When you have successfully moved most of your traffic away from the phone, consider positioning phone as a "value-add" service that includes a per-minute or per-incident charge. As we have discovered, *charging for phone calls has allowed some companies to provide improved, free service through the Web utilizing self-service, chat, and e-mail options.* This is a more serious consideration for post-sales technical support than for an inbound sales line.

The Transition from Self-Service to Live Help

In the traditional call center model when customers make the transition to live help, they generally find themselves in a "start over" mode. The call center agents ask for their name, address, product, request, and more… Companies have developed technology that captures intelligence during the Web session and presents this to the agent. Here is an overview:

- Self-service is never positioned as a hurdle to speaking with a live agent. Within a few easy steps, the customer is presented with a likely solution or answer. If the answer is not apparent or the customer so chooses, the customer may easily transition to a live-agent interaction.

- Before connecting to an agent, the customer inputs information used for easy access (customer name, PIN, etc.) and skills routing (product, problem type, computer OS, and so on). Neither the IVR nor the agent asks the customer for this information again.

- When the customer is connected to the chat agent, *the CRM record is already created and pre-populated with customer information and delivered to the live agent.* In addition to basic information like customer name and their service issue, the entire customer "click stream," plus additional information, is presented to the agent. The click stream provides the agent a "play-by-play" of the screens the customer has visited on the Web site prior to connecting to the live chat agent. Click stream delivery helps the agent understand what the customer was attempting to do, what documents they viewed, etc. This ensures that the agent doesn't ask questions or present information that the customer experienced during the self-service portion of the interaction.

- Some companies, in technical support applications, are able to let the agent automatically view customers' system information including items such as operating system, browser version, products installed, product versions, updates, etc., without asking the customer for this information. Our experience shows that the customer almost never knows this type of information without taking time to look it up, and they usually don't even know where to look.

- When answering customers' questions, the agents provide follow-up e-mail messages with links back to the self-service environment, helping the customer better understand the value of the self-service for future transactions.

This methodology and technology has greatly reduced overall contact center costs, due to lower overall volume, higher resolution rates, and shorter handle time on live interactions. More importantly, *the customer has a better service experience.*

Multimedia Case Management

When the customer contacts a live agent, and there is special software installed, the agent sees the customer's entire Web experience. Instead of the typical entitlement and skills routing process, *the customer is connected to an agent who knows who they are and generally what they want.* Here is how it works:

- When a customer initiates a contact, the customer relationship management record is automatically created and presented to the agent pre-populated with information gathered while the customer navigated the Web site. The agent also sees a record of past interactions from this customer.

- Customers can access and control the status of their open issues. When customers end an interaction with the company contact center, they are presented with an option to open a special e-mail in the instance where their issue was not resolved. When customers return, quick links allow them to review or change the status as well as reconnect to a live agent. The agent receiving the contact—whether by chat, phone, or e-mail—is automatically and immediately presented with the full case record.

- When a customer contact is completed, the customer is automatically presented with a satisfaction survey. Chat or e-mail transcripts, survey results, and agent comments are immediately saved as part of the CRM record.

- This level of integration provides unprecedented reporting capabilities, encompassing the entire customer experience. A CRM record shows the customer's Web site navigation, agent interaction, post-interaction survey, and follow-up interactions regarding the same issue.

This system empowers the customer with the ability to "close the loop" on open issues, or re-open an issue that was thought to be closed. The customer has access to the same tools developed for call-center agents, but limited access to their own account history. Not only does this integrated system lower costs through reduced handle time and increased resolution rates, but it also contributes to an improved customer experience.

Feedback Loop—Continuous Improvement

After each customer interaction, the system presents a quick survey to determine key success factors. Customers rate agent professionalism, issue resolution, and satisfaction with company services. Survey results are tallied daily at the site, team, and individual level. Empirically, we see about a 30% survey-participation rate with customers. Considering that, on average, 80% of all live contacts are by chat; this represents a significant insight into customer satisfaction and loyalty. It is possible to get a statistically sound sampling to the individual agent level, helping quickly identify problem areas and training needs.

Two Case Studies

So far in this chapter we have discussed a proven model and technology for both improving customer service while significantly reducing costs. While some of the elements include traditional call-center work, the greatest and most positive impact on your company's service quality and price will happen by driving customers to effective self-service and Web-based offerings. To illustrate the effectiveness of this service super highway, consider the following results.

NOTE: In both of these case studies, service hours of operation were increased to 24x7, but limited to Web self-service, chat, and e-mail. Phone support was on a fee-basis after hours, but remained free during business hours. Eventually phone was provided on a fee-basis during all hours, but not until 80% of customers had already transitioned to the Web services.

Case Study #1—World Wide Software Solution Provider

In this model, the company successfully reduced their cost by more than 80%

CHALLENGES	RESULTS		
		Before Solution	**After Solution**
• Increasing customer base	**Contacts Per Month:**	88,000	425,000
• Declining product prices	Phone	80,000	25,000
• Uncontrollable customer support costs	Chat/E-mail	8,000	70,000
• Poor customer experience	Self-Help	-	330,000
	ASA:	5 Minutes	1 Minute
• Decreasing customer loyalty	**Support Costs**	$850K per month	$110K per month
• Limited operating hours	**Cost per Contact:**	$7.50	$0.73

A Major Software Company Turns Support Nightmare Into Customer Service Award

A leading software solutions provider is well known for the fact that it fully understands the importance of customer support. Since its inception, the company has made service one of its highest priorities. But providing great support used to be an expensive proposition.

At that time the main vehicle for customer service was free phone support. The company was handling the load, but the invoice for support was as much as 20% of the division's revenue. The Senior Manager of World Wide Consumer Support was ready to investigate some new alternatives.

During this time period the company had also acquired several consumer software houses. What about Web self-service? Were there perhaps some other viable free support alternatives to live support on the phone?

Potentially, one should guide the customer to a series of solutions and at every juncture, offer them the option of live support if they want it. Generally speaking from our observations, if the customer can get a good solution, they'll choose the self-service alternative and will feel good about having done so.

The Senior Manager of World Wide Consumer Support believes it's primarily a matter of giving the customer a good resolution. If the problem gets solved, the customer really doesn't care what the methodology is.

But it's interesting that the team found its greatest opposition to the new ways of thinking from inside. They had a long tradition of providing free phone support 24/7. The company was accustomed to outsourcing its support. But moving from live voice to Web-enabled self-service and chat was a whole new chasm. The senior executive management, and particularly the CIO/CTO executives would have to buy in.

Ironically, as expensive as phone support had become, the senior executives' foremost worry was that the quality of support would slip, or even that the perception of high quality would fall. Those objections were easy to answer. The internal support team was able to show a competitive analysis that proved other similar vendors had already moved away from free phone support, and that the company's new program would be competitively better than theirs. Then they brought out the financial analysis. The World Wide Support Group predicted that the total cost of support would decrease by as much as 40-50 percent. That sealed the decision.

However, the senior executive buy-in wasn't enough.

"Surprisingly, the biggest push-back we got was from our sales force," the Senior Manager of World Wide Consumer Support says. "They were just certain that as soon as word got out we were no longer providing free phone support, they wouldn't be able to sign any deals."

The sales force was the hardest group to convince. And even after the program was up and running in the U.S., there was the separate challenge to convince the teams overseas.

"The European sales teams were especially concerned," he recalls. "They were convinced nobody would use the Web. Certain countries were the hardest of all. In Italy, for example, the lead salesperson kept maintaining that only 12 percent of the population even had access to the Web, and that this idea was destined to fail. Ironically, though, the very countries who complained the loudest were the ones that showed the highest adoption rate after the new campaign was in place."

Ultimately, the company was convinced that they'd have to eliminate free phone support. But the company was determined to still offer its customers some viable solutions for free. On that foundation, the team came back with proposals for the ways that could deliver support primarily over the Web, but would continue to offer fee-based phone support as an alternative.

The outcome was dramatic and immediate. Web support instantly surged to 85 percent of transactions. The initial spike in cost savings was huge—87 percent, which then settled in to a consistent savings of 60-65 percent in overall costs.

"To demonstrate a year-over-year cost reduction of 60 percent is huge. It's amazing," says the Senior Manager of World Wide Consumer Support. "Yet our quality of support has stayed the same and even increased."

Interestingly, while the total customer base has continued to increase, the number of support contacts has stayed relatively flat. The company points out that there's no way of determining how many customers have simply found their own solution in the material posted on the Web.

Since the initial rollout, the Consumer Support Group has continued to fine-tune its programs.

Ultimately, the combination of Web support and live service has had a very happy ending.

The company's support costs have been reduced from $7.50 to $0.73 per transaction. And in October 2002, they serviced 20,000 more customers for $105,000 less than an industry peer, while actually increasing marks for customer satisfaction.

The support challenge that started out as a nightmare is now winning awards. Now that's a happy ending.

Case Study #2: Intuit Corporation—TurboTax Division

Intuit Revolutionizes Customer Support for Turbo Tax with new solutions.

At the end of the 2000 tax season, Intuit's TurboTax division was facing a customer support crisis. Founded in 1983, Intuit has annual revenue of more than $1 billion. The company has nearly 7,000 employees with major offices in 13 states across the U.S. and offices in Canada, Japan and the United Kingdom.

Intuit's TurboTax is the industry's leading software product for enabling consumers to prepare and file their taxes online. The company's customer support issues, of course, spike dramatically around the time that people file their taxes each year.

In 2001, the company's only mechanism for customer support was a phone number that consumers could call when they had questions. The phone service was operational for limited hours, with extended hours on weekends and evenings that consumers could access for an additional fee. That year, TurboTax supported 915,384 transactions. Not surprisingly, the support lines were overwhelmed, the response was poor, and the company's service satisfaction rankings were low.

It was clear that Intuit's seasonal needs created a particularly tough support quandary. The following season, Erik Seone, Director of Service Delivery for TurboTax, held an internal strategy session with his staff. They had decided that Plain Old Telephone Support (POTS) just wouldn't cut it anymore. They had to find a way to give their customers a better option. As they thought through the issues, they mapped out a proposal for a "stepped" solution. They would find a way to guide customers through a series of steps that would help them to either resolve their own issues or, if they were still having problems, to move to the most efficient method of achieving support.

"Within moments, we knew this new model was exactly what we had envisioned," Seoane said.

Seoane's team lobbied hard to get the commitment of management to go forward.

"We had to get the buy in of our top leadership" Seoane says. "Initially, it was hard to convince others that the combination of stepped online services could be the right solution to address the needs of our customers. After all, our traditional model had always been to take care of our customers via the telephone."

The traditional concept of customer support was a barrier as well. Senior executives are accustomed to the concept of providing customers with options. The new model was much more focused on providing solutions, and resolutions, instead.

In 90 days, Intuit was ready to deploy the Customer Choice Platform® it is using today. The solution was up in time to use for the 2001 tax season.

"The results were just dramatic," Seoane says. "We were able to deflect as many as 60 percent of our transactions right off the top. Customers were able to solve their own problems through FAQs and our online knowledge base. And of the 40 percent of remaining transactions, 80-85 percent were helped through chat (offered 24/7), and only 15-20 percent of that remaining group ever required the phone."

"The combination of our online stepped approach (self-help, chat and telephone) and our ability to connect via the Internet, allowed us to triple the number of customers we were able to help during season while keeping our expenses flat year to year."

In all, the solution reduced Intuit's costs from $12.83 to $4.76 per transaction (a savings of 65%). Total transactions rose from 915,384 to 2,761,866 during this time period. Meanwhile, abandonment dropped from 35% to 5%, and the company posted the highest customer satisfaction remarks it has received in 12 years.

But this is far from the end.

As for senior management, they consider the new program a tremendous success. The founder of Intuit, Scott Cook, recently gave Seoane's team the first-ever Intuit Innovation Award, to acknowledge the creativity and the success of their effort.

In the future, Intuit is planning still more innovation. New innovations include passing a cookie from the product to the Web site that helps make support more customized and increasingly more efficient.

"We're integrating the characteristics of our service model into the product itself," Seoane says. "We blur the line between the product and service. Help becomes a much more dynamic and interactive part of the product. I suspect it's the wave of the future. It's pretty exciting."

CHAPTER 7: PITFALLS IN CUSTOMER SELF-SERVICE

To understand the pitfalls in customer self-service, we must first understand the customer's view. Our research shows that customers expect that their self-service experience will:

- be intuitive to use
- be simple to apply
- be faster than assisted service
- be customer-focused, i.e., treat them as an individual
- be successful, namely almost "idiot proof"
- reward them in some way for doing the job themselves

An organization's Web site must be designed in a way that a customer can immediately understand it. The customer's brain shouldn't be overtaxed trying to understand the logic of the site design or contents. It goes without saying that before you launch your site, regular "folks" from outside your organization should test drive it. Observe how quickly they can dive into your site and how easily they can navigate around it. Usability testing is mandatory.

Keep your content simple. Take your cue from the fact that most newspapers are written for a middle school level reader. Those who are charged with writing your site's copy would do well to connect with your customer group so that they have a clear understanding of their audience. This connection could be as simple as silent monitoring phone calls that come into your contact center or listening to tapes of these conversations. Hemmingways and Shakespeares won't do. Employ writers who can explain complex information in an easy-to-understand way.

Oh, we of little patience. Most of us trying to juggle work and family schedules can relate to the need for fast service. Our customers want the right information and content, and they want it now.

With today's technology, there are few excuses (short of a meager budget) for putting information on the Web that isn't current, timely, and relevant to our customers' needs. Anything short of this will leave a customer with a bad impression.

Customers also expect that Web content will be presented in a focused, interactive, and interesting way. They can find sites that offer this elsewhere on the Web if you can't. Figure 7.1 shows a site that may only hold the attention of a patient few. The customer wants to learn more about IRA contribution limits. Many organizations have designed their site so that the customer has to browse through six or more pages to get to the information they need. As the title suggests: three customer clicks and your site may have struck out, i.e., the "least clicks wins."

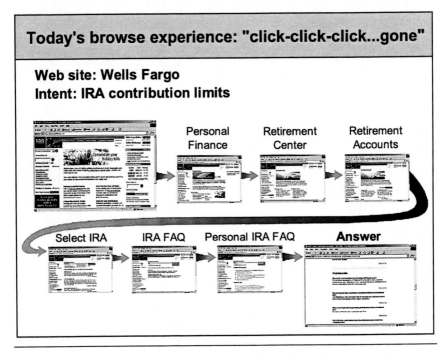

Figure 7.1. Today's browse experience: "click-click-click...gone"

Contrast this site with figure 7.2. When Web self-service is done well, it responds with an exact answer. It offers the customer the opportunity to act on her query and offers guided browsing.

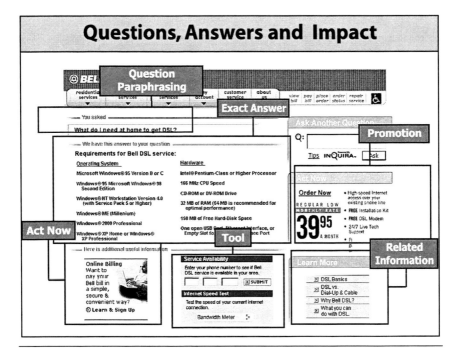

Figure 7.2. Questions, answers and impact

Your Web site content should be driven by the questions that your customers ask most frequently. Customers resent having to plod through marketing-oriented propaganda to find the solutions they need.

Few people, especially potential customers or existing customers, would choose to be frustrated. In general, people want to feel successful. Consider that most of your customers approach your Web site thinking, "I'll try this site, but it'd better work on the first try. If it doesn't work, I've just lost an investment of my time. Then I'll have to go to another channel to get the information I need. I'll have to invest more of my precious time. I won't be a happy camper, if that happens!" When setting the bar for ease of use, realize that many customers approach Web sites with a "one strike and you're out" mentality. For that reason, the self-service stakes are high.

Consider the potential your Web site has to reward your customers. Make sure that your Web site saves them time or money, is convenient, and/or it offers them tangible rewards. Some airlines, for example, offer free miles for those who purchase their ticket on the Web.

Recently, a company called NFO Interactive conducted research on "Online Retail Monitoring, Branding, Segmentation and Web Sites." Customers were asked what would convince them to shop at certain e-tail Web sites. Current online buyers cited the top five reasons they shopped regularly on a particular Web site:

1. I trust that the e-tailer would keep personal information private.

2. The Web site has secure purchasing features.

3. The Web site is technically reliable.

4. The content is up-to-date.

5. The products are delivered on time.

Customers who browsed online but hadn't made any online purchases said that they would consider buying merchandise from an e-tailer that:

- assured them that their privacy would be protected

- offered larger price discounts than offline shops

- enabled them to return products to offline shops (Inc.com, 1999)

Now that we have a clearer understanding of what customers expect from Web self-service, let's consider the pitfalls. They are:

A. Customer behavior is hard to change.

A majority of your customer base needs to be convinced to use self-help options. The biggest reason for the lack of success was that end users didn't adopt either the new technology or a new way of doing business.

Customers are understandably frustrated in their search for information. They hate having to deal with search engines that yield marginally related links. They are dissatisfied by slow e-mail response time and FAQs that are too general to be helpful (Rufo, 2003).

B. Agents may feel threatened.

Your customer service agents might not be good ambassadors of Web self-service. One organization recently reported that its reps purposely sabotaged the initiative because they feared that first-call resolution would go down and call times would increase if all the simple issues were handled by online self-service. You must give your CSRs incentives to be your strongest supporters of Web self-service. They should encourage customers to use it and be willing to educate customers on the system as needed. Take a new look at your contact center metrics. Ensure that they reward CSRs for doing well in the new business environment.

C. Customers may resent being routed through self-service channels.

While the driving force behind Web self-service is customer call-avoidance, your customers cannot be made to feel like impositions. Give the customer choices (see Chapter 6).

D. Customers expect a lot.

Customers expect more information than Web sites are currently prepared to provide.

E. Need more desktop information for complex calls.

With more routine questions and issues being addressed online, CSRs are being asked more complex questions than they have in the past. If organizations don't put more information in the hands of agents, less-experienced ones as well as tenured ones, customers will not get the level of service they expect.

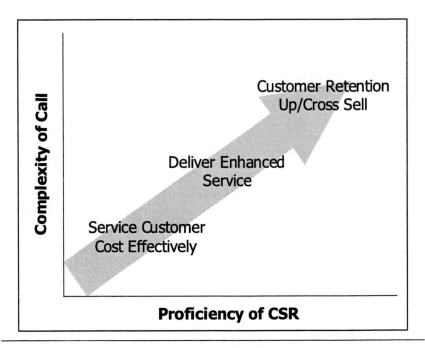

Figure 7.3. Call complexity requires more CSR proficiency

F. Older IT systems can be a problem.

Some organizations discover that the complexity of their information technology (IT) infrastructures puts them at a disadvantage as they seek to implement new technologies to support specific initiatives, such as Web-based initiatives that require them to extend the functionality of their legacy systems to their customers (Hollowell, 2002).

G. Static information can be counter-productive.

Many organizations make the mistake of presenting static information on their initial Web site. Standard information such as phone numbers, addresses, and fixed verbiage from company brochures or other collateral material may have been acceptable in the early days of the Web. This same approach to populating your Web site now can be considered counter-productive. It is essential to keep in mind that customers need solutions to very specific issues. These issues are not typically anticipated by the writers of marketing materials. Also, a company risks losing a customer if it does not regularly update its Web content.

H. Don't offer other channels too quickly.

Those organizations that offer customers the opportunity to hit an e-mail or "Contact Us" button too early on in their Web interaction run the risk of creating a service nightmare. Often times, the unanticipated influx of e-mail quickly overwhelms the limited service staff responsible for replying to them. E-mail responses are delayed or never sent. When the strategy is flawed, the Web becomes a vehicle for customer dissatisfaction and defection.

I. Information must be current.

Some companies make the mistake of relying too heavily on manually managed knowledge bases. These knowledge bases are all too often internally driven. This means that the information might not reflect the real life issues that are on the customers' minds. Without dedicated and continual management, these databases often go out of date. Their content is no longer valid. The customers are dissatisfied with these knowledge bases, and the organizations spend too much time and money to develop and maintain them.

J. Many CRM products.

In a February 2002 InformationWeek.com article, the authors explain another Web self-service pitfall. They noted that, "At this time last year, we were disappointed with CRM product ability to provide robust Web self-service. Most products had limited ability to extend their existing knowledge bases into a Web access model and limited support for integration with third-party knowledge bases. They also had limited capabilities for storing knowledge in a structured fashion to facilitate problem-solving through techniques such as automated suggestion and case-based reasoning." Fortunately, in the last two years, a series of acquisitions and mergers have resulted in better self-service products on the market (Verma and Hollowell, 2002).

K. Customer care is a challenge.

Providing customer care is a challenge in the self-service market. Helping a customer with a problem requires a more complex and less predictable pattern of actions than is required of organizations that sell more straightforward goods or services.

L. Customer communications is key.

Some companies pour money and staff time into a Web self-service option but fail to communicate this offering to their customers. If your Web site fails to draw people away from your live CSRs, you've poured money and time down the drain.

M. A human touch is key.

Some customers miss the human touch. Any issue or question not anticipated for in the rules-based structures of your Web system requires human intervention.

According to Giga Research director John Ragsdale, "Many companies mistakenly think they will cut call volume" when they install online self-service. "That is not necessarily the case." Some companies that we have worked with actually saw their customer inquires more than double. This increase in calls does not necessarily mean that the Web site failed in its mission; it may simply be the result of your site giving you more exposure to potential customers.

N. Knowledge access can be critical.

In a April 2002 ECOMWORLD article, James K. Watson, Jr. warns of another self-service pitfall, "The majority of CRM products offer limited support for integration with knowledge-based vendors, limited availability of the knowledge base across all channels for agents or customers, and limited self-service capabilities for customers and agents to perform advanced and case-based reasoning."

O. Hidden costs are a problem.

Self-service programs can be expensive and laden with hidden expense.

P. Focus on consistent service.

Some contact centers designate a team of CSRs to exclusively handle Internet-based communications. This dual service organization approach means that call center CSRs handle telephone traffic while the Internet CSRs handle Internet traffic. Without close coordination between the two groups, inconsistency of the customer contact can result. It becomes difficult to maintain a single customer contact history. This can often mean that the customer has not been adequately served.

Q. Web-based service required new skills.

Contact center leaders sometimes forget to provide their phone CSRs with the appropriate Internet, typing, and writing skills training they require to serve the customers.

R. Information must be organized to be useful.

With the overwhelming amount of information that exists on even one organization's Web site, it is difficult to organize it effectively.

When considering the pitfalls of Web self-service, leaders cannot ignore the statistics from a June 2000 Forrester report: Ninety-two percent of searches fail to find relevant information or to arrange the results in a meaningful order. Fifty to 80 percent of visitors leave a Web site after a single failed search. More than 60 percent of visitors leave without making a purchase because they couldn't find what they're looking for.

To reap the rewards of Web self-service, and they are considerable, close attention must be paid to the selection, implementation, and process of your Web self-service initiative.

Potentially the best customer service strategy for today's demanding customers is to help customers help themselves in as many ways as possible with self-service. If things don't go well, though, contact centers should be ready to assist customers quickly through assisted self-service. Self-service cannot be force-fed. It is prudent, though, to encourage it as your customer's first option. When customers are allowed to "choose" their preferred channel, companies win, and so do the customers (for actual proof from a case study see Chapter 6).

Just as most IVR self-service applications need live agent backup support, your Web site applications will, too. Customers visiting your Web site need to have a simple, direct way to get from self-service to assisted-service. Most self-service technology available today can track the steps a customer had taken during their online interaction. That means that when the customer's need is escalated, the service rep will know what the customer is trying to accomplish. By giving customers an easy-to-locate outlet that will ensure those needs get met, you are increasing your chances of the customer trying self-service again.

We define seamless assisted self-service as "any solution that allows a customer who has first tried self-service to seamlessly transition to a live agent without the loss of information already provided by the customer." Examples of assisted self-service include allowing a visitor to your Web site several escalate options:

- to e-mail
- to connect to a chat group
- to select a "call me" button for help
- to connect to the "voice of the Internet," which is also known as VOIP

The goals of self-service integrated with assisted self-service are to:

- Allow customers to handle "low value" transactions through self-service options. These types of transactions are those that don't increase customer loyalty to your organization and/or don't result in increased revenue. They can be simple requests for information, or simple "change my address" actions.

- Minimize the use of "high value" live agents for low value transactions. Realizing this kind of goal can often mean a reduction in staff attrition, because CSRs are relieved of the boredom that comes from answering the same, simple inquiries over and over again. It can also mean that your top talent is not wasted. This select group of service reps can be put to better use.

- Maximize the use of high value live CSRs for high value transactions such as sales opportunities, up- and cross-sell opportunities, and/or handling problems and complaints.

When a contact center successfully plans for and implements an effective self-service and assisted-service initiative, the results are significant. The organization retains control over the service delivery system. You can choose which assisted-service options make most sense for your staff and budget. You decrease the chances of the customer picking up the phone to resolve his/her issue, the most costly option from a contact center perspective.

With assisted self-service, the customer history transfers from the customer's first point of contact to his/her next point of contact. This helps decrease the customer's dissatisfaction as s/he is not put in a position to have to retell his/her story.

Assisted self-service also removes the double-penalty of time. The double-penalty stems from the fact that it takes time to "try" self-service, and if it doesn't work, you would normally have to get in line again to wait for the assisted-service. In the proper design, the customers who try self service are rewarded by immediate access to assisted-service with all the information automatically transferred to the live agent.

Another benefit of assisted self-service is that your CSR can use the opportunity to educate the customer on self-service through co-browse activities. A great example of this is the current use of kiosks at airports to get boarding passes. If the passenger needs help (assisted-service), the agent immediately comes over and helps. In the process the agent can educate the passenger in all aspects of this do-it-yourself process, and thereby ensure that the passenger will use the kiosk self-service the next time, and most probably, be successful without further assistance. In the migration from live calls to self-service on the Web site, we can learn a lot by observing what the airlines are doing with the self-service kiosk at the airport.

When done well, the integration of Web self-service with assisted-service results in call and e-mail deflection. This reduces your costs substantially while improving customer satisfaction. Improvements in customer satisfaction, in turn, increase customer loyalty, which typically means an increase in bottom line profits. Have we got your attention now?

As you consider which contacts lend themself best to self-service, consider the following questions as potential pains to fix, or as opportunity detectors:

1. Do your customers have to wait to achieve any of their needs? (Customers hate to wait!)

   Examples might be:

   - Do they have to wait in a line?
   - Do they have to wait until the company is open?
   - Do they have to wait while you look something up for them?
   - Do they have to wait for you to re-order, re-stock, etc.?

2. Do your customers have to fill out paperwork? (Customers hate paperwork!)

   Examples might be:

   - Do they have to complete forms that were completed previously?
   - Do they have to volunteer information that they know is already in your computer?
   - Are your forms clear and friendly?

3. How easy is it for your customer to use your product or service? (Customers don't like complex products!)

   Examples might be:

   - Do they have to read a manual to operate the product?
   - Are most functions and features intuitively obvious to the average casual user?

4. How easy is it to do business with your company? (Customers don't like hassles!)

   Examples might be:

   - Are they frequently referred to your company's policies?
   - Are they assigned only one person to deal with for ordering products?
   - Is it easy to return unwanted products?
   - Are product warranty claims easily processed and paid?

Lastly, as you begin to select one self-service option over another in terms of possible reengineering opportunities, try to gauge each initiative on one or more of the following criteria:

1. How much time would the resulting self-service option save the customer? (Customers love to save time!)
2. How much money would the resulting self-service option save the customer? (Customers love to save money!)
3. How would the self-service option affect your head count? (Companies love to reduce full-time equivalents!)
4. How much money does the self-service option save your company? (Companies love to save money, too!) (Anton, 1996)

One of the most potent advantages to an integrated Web self- and assisted-service initiative is your ability to ensure your customers a seamless service interaction while using only the most cost effective level of support necessary for that interaction. A vice president from your most lucrative account who tries to use your Web site should get the highest possible level of service and be able to promptly access every part of your system. On the other hand, a new customer might be adequately served with fewer resources. This brings us to the need for your organization to devise a cohesive self- and assisted-service strategy.

Introduction

To obtain the level of service you need to create and/or keep a base of loyal customers, you will need to be strategic in your approach to self- and assisted-service. In order to determine where your organization needs to focus improvement efforts in terms of Web service, consider the following questions:

- Do you supply maps and directions on your Web site so that customers can find retailers or distributors in their area?

- Does your Web site enable your customers to quickly find solutions to their most frequently asked queries?

- Does your Web site have a "natural language" search engine?

- Is the information most requested and/or most useful to your customers presented first on your Web site?

- Can your customers easily check on the status of your reply to their previous inquiries?

- Do you reply to customer e-mail inquiries within 24 hours?

- Are your live CSRs easily accessible to those Web customers who cannot find resolution to their issue on your site?

- Can your CSRs help customers navigate through your Web site by actually monitoring and/or taking control of their live sessions?

- Are your customers frequent visitors to your Web site? Do you have the means to determine whether they are or not?

- Can you produce weekly reports that detail the activities that have occurred on your Web site? Do these reports help your organization calculate the site's return on investment (ROI)?

- Do customers ever provide positive feedback regarding their experience using your site?

- Do your customers have the option to request your organization's updates automatically via e-mail?

- Are you regularly mining the wealth of information that resides in the minds of your best CSRs? Do you capture and publish information on your Web site that would be useful to customers?
- Does your site's content automatically grow based on customer input?
- Has your call volume been reduced? Have you deflected telephone calls to live CSRs that can be managed via self-service on your Web site?

If you answered "yes" to most of these questions, from an e-service perspective, your organization is in good shape. If you answered more negatively than positively, you're not alone. Even more importantly, you're right where you need to be—reading this book.

In a May 2002 article titled *Holding These Truths to be CRM Self-service,* Forrester principal analyst Bruce Temkin shares his insight about implementing a self-service strategy. He warns, "...some businesses are haphazard about implementation of the self-service CRM applications they already have purchased. Many self-service strategies lack focus, good practices and integration with other channels. Since it's really still early for self-service, many companies mismanage the operational nuances, like not appropriately merchandising their self-service or, even worse, burying it within their sites." The writer of the article shares that Temkin believes businesses will learn from their mistakes and get wiser about where and how to use self-service technology (Caisse, 2002).

Implementing Web self-service or improving your current offering is much like the implementation or upgrading of any other software project. The potential for success hinges on a number of essential steps. These steps include:

- Define business objectives
- Identify, involve, and communicate with all internal stakeholders
- Conduct a comprehensive needs assessment
- Gain a thorough knowledge of the capabilities of the technology and the vendor

- Design an implementation plan that includes actions, targeted completion dates, and party or parties responsible for each
- Measure organization's and competitors' current performance to establish baseline measurements
- Implement a pilot program prior to launch
- Measure service gains via user feedback and make course adjustments
- Market your site to all internal and external stakeholders

With these planning components in place, you'll increase your organization's chances of achieving Web self-service, assisted-service, and overall service success.

According to a March 2002 Gartner Report, "Implementing Web self-service for customer service can yield reduced costs for customer maintenance. However, it has to be properly implemented and this starts with proper planning. Planning for Web self-service systems in conjunction with the customer service strategy, while ensuring that the system will be utilized, yields the benefits organizations seek" (Perez, 2002). That brings us to the next chapter where we'll discuss each of these planning steps in detail.

CHAPTER 10: PLANNING YOUR WEB-BASED CUSTOMER SERVICE STRATEGY

Previous chapters have included the background information you need in order to deliberately consider the way your organization views customer service. We have looked at the driving forces behind the increased call for Web self-service. Customers' expectations, including their potential pain points, have been put forward. The advantages of technology improvements have been compared to the investment of large sums of money in recruiting, hiring, and training staff members. We have also cautioned against the pitfalls of Web self-service that every organization would like to avoid. Now that we're all on the same page, let's dig into the planning work that's required to implement an effective Web self-service strategy.

Self-service Solution Providers

In a recent study of our twelve thousand plus member benchmark community we asked which packaged self-service application did they have in place. The following is a list of those solution providers:

Amdocs	InQuira
Divine	Jeeves Solutions
eAssist	Kana
eDocs	Mercado
eGain	Onyx
Epicor	Vantive
Firepond	

Define Business Objectives

To get started, study a mapping of your organization's current processes. Consider in simplest terms what it is you want to achieve. Ask yourself the following questions:

- What are the customer desired outcomes for each mapped out process?

- What should our customers' service experience look and sound like?

- How does that vision compare to what our customers are currently experiencing?
- How does our service stack up against customer expectations?
- Are we easy to communicate with?
- What customer complaints do we hear most frequently?
- What would it take to prevent those complaints?
- How does our service stack up against the competition?
- What would it take to surpass customer expectations?

Our opinion of what a high-level Web interaction platform might include is depicted in figure 10.1.

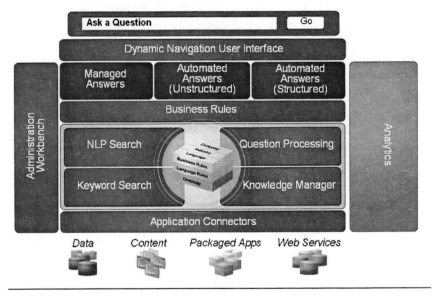

Figure 10.1. Web interaction platform

These lists are not all-inclusive. Ideally, though, they will launch a discussion that will help you nail down what it is you want to accomplish. Take notes, and categorize ideas once you feel as though you've thoroughly covered the scope of issues that need your organization's attention. Prioritize the ideas, making your top priorities those that should result in the most effective change and/or those that will likely result in the greatest ROI.

Identify, Involve, and Communicate with all Internal Stakeholders

While business leaders have the responsibility of setting the organization's course direction and corresponding priorities, be aware that a gold mine of information exists within your organization. Your employee pool and their collective experience and knowledge is that gold mine.

Consider which departments of your organization will play a role in helping to achieve the business objectives you've established. To determine who these employee groups are, follow your existing processes and identify the process owners. These process owners are your stakeholders.

By involving and communicating with stakeholders, you will accomplish a number of things. Assuming you're open to it, you will likely gain a clearer picture of the actual terrain over which your organization will need to navigate. You will likely get valuable input that you may not have considered. And, equally important, you will increase your chances of getting these stakeholders' buy-in. The value of this buy-in cannot be overestimated. It has the power to propel or sabotage your objectives. Don't forget to communicate frequently with this group. Communicate objectives, changes, progress updates, the need for additional input, etc.

Conduct a Comprehensive Needs Assessment

Your stakeholders, identified earlier, will help you determine what knowledge will be needed to improve each of the processes you identified. They should also be able to help you identify where that knowledge resides.

Determine the degree of self-maintenance your customers are prepared for. Begin by assessing your customer base to identify skill sets, knowledge levels and current technology employed. With this knowledge, choose and implement delivery systems and processes that your customers will be most comfortable with. By choosing technologies compatible with the systems the majority of your customers currently utilize, you can speed the adoption curve by reducing the objections they may have regarding cost and implementation issues.

Gain a Thorough Knowledge of the Technology's and Vendor's Capabilities

Select and manage your tools and offerings carefully. Usage of modems, public electronic-mail, voice response systems, computer telephony integration, wide-area networks, and the Internet, is increasing at dramatic rates in both the corporate and consumer marketplaces. To take advantage of this change in customer behavior and expectations, it is critical that you provide them with the necessary tools to make this transition successful. Being on the forefront of the paradigm shift to client/server will help you choose the right technology infrastructure to provide the tools which will most rapidly benefit your customers.

The importance of choosing the appropriate vendor and technology cannot be overstated. As you consider your options, consider the following criteria:

1. Does the technology provide adequate functionality to meet your business needs? For example, organizations with helpdesks should make sure that the technology supports remote diagnostics and repair. Similarly, organizations that want text chat and/or co-browsing options should ensure the technology offers those capabilities. Also, the technology should support the integration of all interaction channels (from telephone to e-mail) to ensure the customer seamless service. To increase the accuracy of customer resolutions, you should ensure all your solutions are being supported by a common knowledge base.

2. Is the solution time tested? Chances of the technology adequately meeting your organizational needs typically increase after multiple releases. The product stability and functionality tends to increase over time.

3. Does the technology integrate with your existing contact center routing technologies and infrastructure? Does it enable the blending of phone and Web interfaces so that numerous customers can be served at one time through one service rep port?

4. Can the technology support highly personalized and/or highly complex Web sites? Is it flexible? Can it provide management of service rep access to user screen and user desktop?

5. Does the technology have the ability to support heavy user loads? The system should be able to scale up under heavy loads as is often necessary in large corporations and/or during seasonal business peaks.

6. Does the technology allow you to serve your entire customer base? Does it support all of the languages that your customers speak?

7. Will the technology allow supervisors to monitor agent productivity and effectiveness? Will it allow simultaneous chat sessions? Can supervisors monitor chat conversations and "whisper" information to the service rep to help offer an effective resolution?

8. Will the technology work in highly secured electronic environments? Will it work properly across firewall protection?

9. Does the technology allow for seamless customer escalation?

10. Will the technology have the capability to interface with databases across the organization? It is essential that it supports unified customer service across communication channels and service reps. It is key that the technology leverages customer information and organization-wide knowledge to the fullest.

As you weigh different technologies, consider the needs of your customers. Then compare how well those needs will be met by managed answers versus structured retrieval versus an intelligent search. The following figure compares the three.

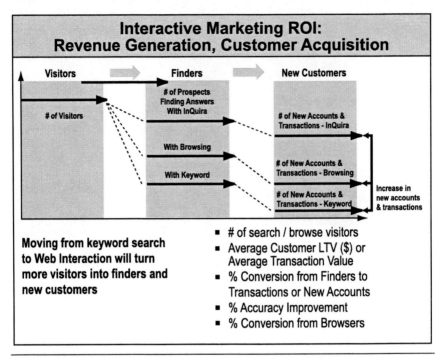

Figure 10.2. Interactive marketing ROI: revenue generation, customer acquisition

11. Can the vendor provide you with product and service endorsements from companies that have had similar technology requirements? What proof do you have that the vendor has successfully implemented the kind of technology you need?

Design an Implementation Plan

Design an implementation plan that includes actions, targeted completion dates, and the party or parties responsible for each.

Begin the drafting of this plan by determining the expected implementation date. This date may be driven by customer expectations, marketing needs, and/or simply by the whims of corporate leadership. Once the date is established, work backwards to plot out each step that will need to happen in order to ensure a successful implementation. Decide which person or committee is responsible for each step, and commit to deadlines for each. Establish a system for regularly updating all internal stakeholders on the progress of the project.

Clear and frequent communication will be key to a successful implementation. Set expectations for responsible parties in writing, as well as verbally communicating them.

Establish Baseline Measurements

Measure the organization's and competitors' current performance to establish baseline measurements.

Consider how you will measure success. Will success be measured in the total number of e-mail, chat, or phone contacts? Will it be in ratios of each of these to the total number of contacts? Will you measure success in revenue generated? In cost containment? In call avoidance? If you choose to measure success through call avoidance, you can simply compare historical call volume with future call volume.

Whatever criteria you use to measure baseline performance will be the same criteria that are measured after the implementation of the new technology, processes, and training. The comparison of the two sets of data will provide you with a gauge by which to judge your success.

We also believe it's important to benchmark your competition before you launch a new or improved Web self-service and assisted-service program (or any other project of consequence, for that matter). Benchmarking will provide you reference points outside your business that will indicate what it will take to get ahead and/or remain ahead of your competition. In the process of benchmarking, you'll get an accurate "picture" of your current operation which can be compared with a benchmark after launching the new Web-based self-service initiative.

Measure Service Gains via User Feedback and Make Course Adjustments

Use the tracking and analysis capabilities of your customer information system to track usage and success rates of customer self-service. Today's advanced customer information systems, such as Siebel and InQuira, provide sophisticated tracking and reporting capabilities which provide valuable information on how even the largest, most complex customers use your empowerment tools to increase their self-maintenance ability. By linking to complementary technologies such as automatic call distributors (ACDs), voice response systems and fax-back systems, you can encourage and reward customers who embrace the self-maintenance trend. Additionally, develop a ROI formula to measure the impact of these investments in empowerment on both the company and your customers. Build your cost and revenue models with complete data. Consider all direct and indirect delivery costs, including all facets (marketing, administrative, finance, information systems) involved in creating, communicating, delivering and accounting for the offerings.

The following illustration shows you the type of system metrics that the best vendors are able to offer. These reports will make measuring the return on your investment easier.

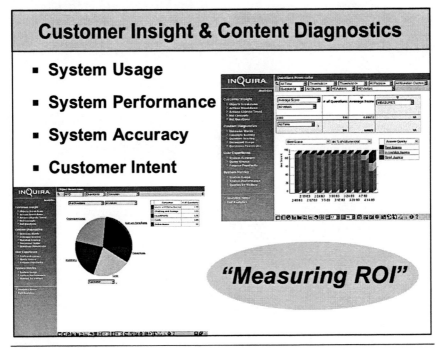

Figure 10.3. System reports on performance metrics

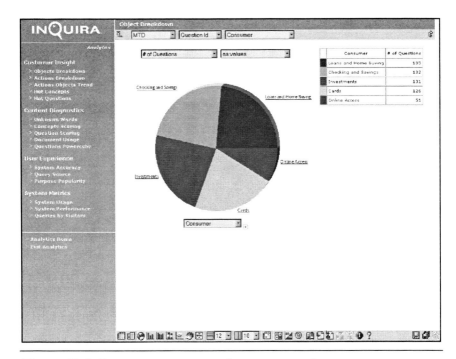

Figure 10.4. System reports on performance metrics

Your customer information infrastructure should also enable you to easily poll your customer base and test their satisfaction with service performance and results. Use this information to evaluate your self-maintenance offerings, modify them when necessary, and ensure the continued success of your service contracts.

Market Your Site to all Internal and External Stakeholders

Market and sell your program internally. Prior to launching the programs, invest the time to educate everyone who sells to, or supports customers, and how they may use the new program. Marketing and sales personnel need to be well equipped to position the self-service programs properly, respond confidently to objections and explain the benefits, criteria and investments for each program. In addition to understanding and being comfortable discussing the offerings, sales and support personnel need to know specifically what customers will be able to do and how they may need to modify their behavior. For example, if historically only employees who captured service call information were able to read comments entered in the database, it may be necessary to remind them that customers will now be able to read what they record. As a result, service personnel should be advised that under no circumstances should they include in the database emotionally charged observations about a customer.

Market and sell your program externally. Market your programs as you would any other products or services offered by your company. Educate potential customers on the benefits, fees, and ways to use the new program. Share the reason for the change, the impact it will have on them, and how they can take advantage of it. Highlight the benefits and cost differences between these offerings and current offerings. If adoption of the new program requires special equipment or additional product modifications, offer them at a significantly reduced rate, or, if possible, at no charge. Create processes which welcome new users of the programs as soon as possible after they've experienced the tool. Create procedures which guarantee a positive experience the first time a customer uses the program. And don't forget to promote your successes! The more aware customers are of the frequency they've used your services and results of that usage, the more likely they are to use the service again, bringing them ever closer to making it their primary method for assistance.

The key to successful self and assisted-service requires more than selecting and implementing the best technology. It also requires a the company's team to learn from industry best practices.

Ensure that Someone "owns" Your Web Self- and Assisted-service

The long-term owner need not be the executive or manager who launched it. This owner should, however, fully understand your business needs and the business objectives behind the launching or improvement of your Web self-service and assisted-service initiative.

E-service initiatives are ever-changing. To be successful, they must adapt to the changing needs of your organization and your customers. They must also adapt as new services and/or products are launched, as new markets and technologies evolve, and the use of your Web site increases. All of this adaptation requires an "owner-like" commitment.

This owner will act as cheerleader and change agent. He or she will provide direction and accountability for the project to ensure that organizational support for it does not diminish.

From our experience, the most successful first-wave adopters of self-service have—almost without exception—had very strong champions leading the way.

Ensure Cross-departmental Collaboration

It is essential to the success of your self-service initiative that it is fully supported by all internal stakeholders. Effective e-service content and processes depend on the active participation and commitment of this diverse group of people.

Your stakeholders will typically include representatives from a variety of departments. This group may include representatives from customer service, marketing, technical support, accounting, sales, shipping, and the Web site administer. Some organizations may even want to include in this group its suppliers and distributors. One person may "own" the site (as described above), another may administer it, while others may produce much of the content. This group's commitment to the Web site and each member's ability to collaborate with one other is essential.

When recruiting and motivating this core group of stakeholders, be sure you appeal to their self-interest. The marketing stakeholder, for example, will benefit by the success of the Web project. He or she can use the organization's site to cross-sell and up-sell electronically. No matter who is involved in this group, every site owner should ensure that from the beginning he or she has the commitment and help from those needed throughout the planning, implementation, and maintenance stages. The fewer surprises for your stakeholders, the better for them and you.

Commit to Continuous Improvement

Some software vendors suggest that diligent self-service managers have the ability to increase their organization's ROI by 200 percent and more after implementing Web self-service technology. The key word here is *diligent*. Because self-service technology tends to deliver significant benefits very early on after implementation, some organizations can become lax once it's up and running. They become satisfied with a self-service ROI rate of 60-70 percent.

While a 60-70 percent return rate is valuable, there is much more room for improvement—much more ROI just waiting to be realized. Self-service technology typically has built-in feedback mechanisms. Those tenacious self-service managers who focus on continuous improvement will want to utilize customer comments regarding site contents and site traffic data, both of which are available to them as part of the technology capabilities. By tapping into this type of feedback and turning this feedback into improvement initiatives, managers can increase the technology's benefit to the organization.

The following figure emphasizes the importance of continuous improvement of your Web self-service site. The commitment to continually improve will enable your organization to meet customer and business objectives. Those organizations that do not pay enough attention to continuous improvement may meet customer and business short term objectives but will likely fail to meet the long term objectives of either segment.

What is effective Web self-service and interactive marketing?

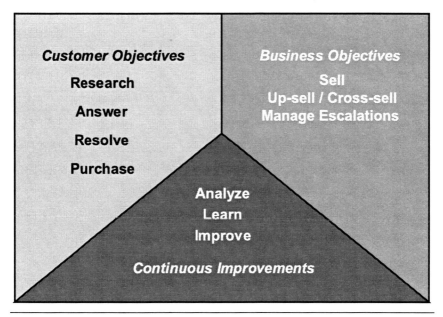

Figure 11.1. What is effective Web self-service and interactive marketing?

Offer Helpful Knowledge Items Quickly

Sounds basic. Doesn't it? Yet when it comes to site design and navigation, many self-service implementers overlook some of the simplest truths.

The sooner your site can get customers the knowledge items they need, the better. Ideally, your solution will have clearly label links on your company's home page. These links can be identified as "Need help?," "Customer Service," "Questions?," etc. Whichever link label you choose, your customer should be led directly to a list of top ten answers.

Surprisingly, some self-service implementers nest essential content within other areas of their site. Customers can't find the solution to their question and/or problem on their own and don't realize that it's even on the site. This mistake results in customer e-mails or phone calls to live service reps—just what you are trying to avoid.

Another mistake you want to avoid is requiring your customers to navigate through one or more layers of knowledge categories before they can find the solution they need. Your customers want to see answers **immediately**. Since the majority of their needs can be met with a small number of knowledge items, make every effort to present those knowledge items as quickly as possible. If the knowledge items you've listed don't meet the customers' needs, they can continue their search. They now see what your site's knowledge items look like and will likely continue searching with more assurance that they'll be able to find what they're looking for.

Display Site Content Before Company Phone Numbers and E-mail Address

While conventional wisdom may say it's good service to list your organization's toll free telephone number prominently on your Web site, we advise against it. We suggest your "Contact us" link, whether that connects customers to an e-mail form or a live service rep, not be displayed until **after** your customers have seen at least one knowledge item from your Web site. Let them enter the site and attempt self-service before they have ready access to phone or e-mail channels.

While this approach may not seem customer-friendly, we believe it is. Assume that customers come to your site to find an answer or resolution. Your site design can facilitate them finding their answer or resolution on their own, at their convenience. No queues to wait in, no busy signals, no reliance on a service rep. We believe that once your customers experience that first positive self-service interaction, you've hooked them. And the more customers that are hooked on self-service, the more you'll decrease your service and support costs. We see it as a win/win.

As the following Web site graphic illustrates, the "Contact Us" link is not displayed prominently. The most significant display is open space for the customer to list her question. Also displayed prominently are the most Frequently Asked Questions. This site setup will likely be more effective in deflecting calls from the organization's telephone service reps than those that list the "Contact Us" link more prominently. The organization saves money; the customer saves time.

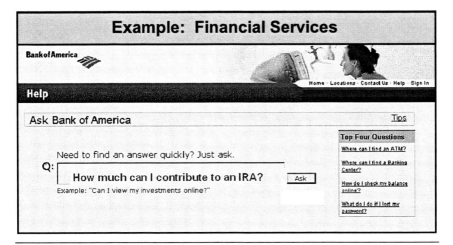

Figure 11.2. Example: display FAQ's

Provide Customers with Everything They Need Within the Service Section of Your Company Web Site

Your corporate Web site may contain product information in one section, shipping information in another, and return policies in yet another section. For customer convenience and to increase the effectiveness of your site, all information like this should be displayed in the service section. Once customers enter this section, they should not have to exit it to search elsewhere to find what they need.

It's well worth your time to review your organization's Web content. Ask yourself if there's any information on your site that could be used as an answer to a FAQ. Include as much information as possible in the service section of your site. This re-positioning of existing content can significantly improve self-service usage rates and improve customer satisfaction. Another win/win!

Ensure Your Site is Visual and Interactive

One of the greatest advantages of Web self-service over phone service is the Web's visual nature. While well-written Web content is essential to a successful site, many customers appreciate the photos, diagrams, and streaming videos that they can't get from phone service. Many companies that sell technical products offer diagrams on their Web sites that walk customers through a repair one click at a time.

Often, the kind of visual content that would benefit your customers already exists. Consider any computer-based training or online manuals your organization owns. If you have the luxury of already having this material in house, all you need to do is get those visuals to the service section of your Web site. Best case scenario: make it an answer to a FAQ. Even if it is necessary to develop visuals to upgrade the quality of your site, it is typically well worth the cost and effort. Often the cost can be justified once you consider the number of phone calls and e-mails that were generated by customers' confusion over topics that weren't previously supported by visuals.

Be Liberal with Links

Not all your customers visit your Web site looking for help. They may happen across your site or they may simply be shopping. They may encounter an issue that becomes a question they'd like answered. Their question may be related to a process or feature on the site itself. For your customer's convenience and your organization's best interest, include prominent links back to your site's service section in many places. We'd go so far as to recommend that you strategically place some kind of a "Need Help?" link back to service in a consistent place throughout your site. This is your first line of defense when it comes to call avoidance. You are, in essence, training your customers to first try to help themselves rather than calling in or sending an e-mail.

Market Your Web Self-service

Because PCs are typically so prevalent in your customers' homes and in their offices, it's likely that they are in front of their computer as they wait in your organization's telephone service queue. Use this "captive audience" time to suggest they use your Web self-service option. Market this service to them via your contact center's hold messages. Chances are that many of your customers will be able to solve their own issues as they wait in queue.

Your service reps can also market your Web self-service option each time they recognize the information they're providing the customer is available via self-service. Our only caution with this kind of marketing is that your service reps be sure to promptly and politely provide the customer resolution. Then they can explain to the customer where this information appears on your Web site and the customer advantages to Web self-service. Service reps must be careful not to show irritation with these customers or give the customers the feeling that they are imposing on your organization.

Give Your Self-service Customers an Easy Out

You want to reinforce your customers' behavior each time they use Web self-service. You don't want to draw them into your site and make them feel trapped there. While we recommended earlier that you do not display phone or e-mail options before your customers see your online content, the customer's option to be in contact with a service rep must be always be offered within your service section. You have the option to offer phone service, e-mail, real-time chat, or a combination of these. Just ensure you offer at least one immediate contact option.

One company we worked with actually monitors how long a customer is on their Web site, and after five minutes has passed, they pro-actively present the visitor with a chat window that says, "how can we assist you in your current search for information?"

Often this "easy out" leaves you in some control of your customer's inquiry. You can offer them less expensive options than phone service, such as e-mail and chat. If you fail to offer this "easy out" option, you not only run the risk of frustrating and angering your customer, you also are more likely to get a high volume of phone calls into your contact center, unfortunately, the most expensive option for your contact center to handle.

Consider Buying Software that Automatically Suggests Answers to E-mails Before They're Sent

It is not unusual for customers to launch an e-mail from an organization's Web site without realizing the solution to their question or issue is within your site. You can save company resources by purchasing software that automatically suggests to the customer pertinent knowledge items from your database. Each time this automation adequately addresses the customer's issue, you save your organization the cost of having a service rep manually answer the inquiry. And you're also encouraging your customers to find their own resolution in future Web site visits.

Take Advantage of Escalation and Flexible Workflow Functions

If it is a priority for your organization to reply to e-mails within 24 hours, you can purchase software that supports this goal. Workflow rules can be used to alert your service supervisors to e-mails that have gone 18 hours without resolution. This allows your service staff time to meet your organizational goal of ensuring customer satisfaction.

Some of today's more sophisticated software can even spot emotional cues each time a customer is particularly dissatisfied with your service. Exclamation points and/or specific words of anger are automatically "recognized." These messages can be automatically flagged to ensure your most competent service reps handle them.

When you combine the appropriate software for your organization with these best practices, we believe you'll see amazing results and a significant ROI in little time.

CHAPTER 12: THE PEOPLE SIDE OF THE EQUATION: EMPLOYEES AND CUSTOMERS

In recent years, the call center has moved from a back-office cost center to the front line of the corporate customer relationship management, or CRM, strategy. Technology has allowed us to open many additional channels of communication between customers and organizations. In effect, many call centers have evolved into more versatile and sophisticated **contact centers**.

In order to fully realize the potential of these contact centers, leaders must not only rethink their existing technology and processes, they must rethink the people side of the equation as well. Specifically, prudent leaders are taking a more strategic view of their service employees and customer base. This chapter will focus on the increasing importance of transforming the CSR into a Knowledge Worker. We will also look at the need to identify customer segments and match each with appropriate service level offerings.

The fact is, that in previous chapters we have focused on allowing the customer self-service access to information on the company's Web site, however, the agent often has the same information needs. Therefore, having a natural language search ability for customers is just as useful for the customer service agent who may be dealing with a caller that is not Web-enabled yet needs the same information. This leads us to the new concept of an agent being a person that dispenses knowledge, i.e., a knowledge worker.

Transform the CSR into a Knowledge Worker

In the transition from call center to contact center, organizations have increasingly realized that the profile of those on the frontlines of service must change. Successful service organizations have moved from hiring individuals with minimum skills at minimum pay to recruiting more sophisticated knowledge workers.

In a June 2002 article, Esteban Kolsky from the Gartner Group, says, "Even though there's a fantasy that self-service reduces the quantity of calls coming into agents, self-service really affects the quality of the calls. Since basic information can now be provided through Web delivery, agents are getting more complex calls, which requires more advanced knowledge of the company and its products and services. Each agent, therefore, needs to be more of a knowledge worker."

The challenge for many organizations today is to capture employees' knowledge and share it across the organization. Those who do this effectively transform their employees into knowledge workers. When you consider the potential depth and breadth of this collective body of information, you begin to understand what is to be gained by making the best use of it. But the trick is that only when this information is collected into a single database and organized effectively, can its potential be fully unleashed.

Kolsky was asked what CRM and e-service vendors need to do to help Web self-service become a success, he suggests that, "Vendors...need to bring knowledge management into the CRM world. Organizations are finally realizing that the most valuable information resides in an unstructured format—in the brains of their employees, in community forums, and in chat and e-mail sessions. Knowledge management tools are the only way to capture and structure that information so that it can be re-used."

Organizations are beginning to understand that the maintenance of separate information systems and silos of departmental files is counterproductive. Many, more savvy organizations, understand that they are better served by the development of open Web-based technologies that enable easy integration among applications, devices, and data storage. As is quoted in a 2002 *Microsoft Insight* article, "Technology is the knowledge worker's enabler." (Microsoft, 2002)

In the current information age, the old saying "knowledge is power" is more accurate than ever before. The Delphi Group found that service employees spent "30 percent of their time just searching for information." Issue resolutions are delayed, work is redundant, and productivity slips. It doesn't take a math whiz to realize the enormous price tag that is attached to the ineffective organization of information. The Delphi Group calculated this cost. Assuming a fully loaded cost of $120,000 per knowledge worker (total center cost divided by total FTEs), the group suggested that approximately $36,000 per employee is wasted annually. They extrapolate from there. "Improving that 30 percent by even five percentage points to 25 percent can result in savings of $6,000 per employee per year. In an organization with 500 employees, that's over $3 million savings annually."

It is essential that organizations be aware of the limitations, challenges, and needs of today's knowledge workers. These workers:

- Get frustrated when they have to navigate through many different interfaces to find the information they seek.
- Don't always know where to look for the resolutions they are seeking or even how to ask for them.
- Want and need broad access to organizational information whether it is in the form of documents, applications, or data.
- Need tools to help them filter through large amounts of data to find the pertinent information they need to make the best decisions they can.

At one high-tech customer support center, the agent proudly told us "All the knowledge I needs is right here at my fingertips." She went on to painfully explain, "The challenge is which finger to use."

Your organization's support systems should facilitate knowledge workers' ability to do their jobs. The systems should result in higher productivity, decreased costs, and higher employee satisfaction rates. When the systems don't live up to their potential, you will notice business implications such as:

- Declining employee productivity because your knowledge workers can't readily find the information they need.
- Increased costs when your knowledge workers look to more expensive information avenues such as meetings, phone calls, or outside consultants.
- Increased employee frustration due to the difficulty of finding information necessary to do their jobs properly.
- ROI suffers.

Self-service search and navigation technology exists today which is designed to meet the needs of knowledge workers. The goal of this technology is to leverage all company information and provide a more effective search experience to those who need it the most—your knowledge workers. When an organization is equipped with a more sophisticated knowledge base, it will benefit in a number of ways. Training costs will likely be reduced because knowledge workers will have less information to learn and retain. They will instead need to know how to search for the information they need. The more robust the knowledge base is and the better organized it is, the less training will be required. Your frontline staff will also be equipped to work more productively and to make more informed business decisions.

A number of vendors also offer a feature where search results can be tailored to that employee's level of entitlement. New technology ensures the right knowledge worker gets the right information at the right place and the right time.

The *Microsoft Insight* article quoted above lists the benefits of this new technology. Used strategically, it can:

- Empower employees to quickly and easily manage, access, create, share, and act on information any time, any place and on any device. Employees should have single-click access to analytical and collaborative tools; database and data analysis on desktop and mobile devices; and a unified tool for calendar, e-mail, and task synchronization and management, accessible from all devices.

- Provide "customer centric" services by enabling employees to respond to customers more quickly and effectively. This requires database and data analysis across multiple channels.

- Increase organizational IQ through collaboration, by integrating content management, tracking and analysis systems. This involves easy-to-use and easy-to-manage development tools, integration with back-office and legacy systems, and high levels of security and authentication to protect departmental data.

The value of an integrated service delivery system that turns CSRs into knowledge workers cannot be overstated. When information is easy to access, your staff is more likely to search for it. Your staff is also more likely to use the knowledge and expertise of others if those colleagues are easy to contact. Your staff is also more likely to follow your organization's protocol if it is easy to follow. Web-based communication acts as a catalyst for knowledge workers to address their customers' issues directly, to provide accurate resolution, and to treat customers as they should be treated rather than as a nuisance.

Identify Customer Segments and Match Each with Appropriate Service Level Offerings

Different organizations will likely measure their Web self-service success differently. While many organizations once measured success by the number of hits their Web site received, in today's economy, this is likely not a wise measure of success for any organization.

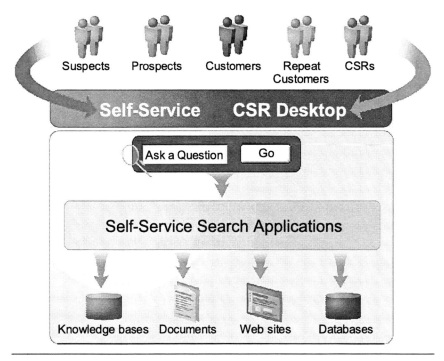

Figure 12.1. A single touch point for managing knowledge access

A better measure of success, for an e-tailer for example, might be the organization's ability to retain customers and convert them into habitual buyers. We have seen statistics that show that 75 percent of all Internet sales are made by 25 percent of Internet users (CommerceNet, Oct 1999). The ability to identify and reach this core group of buyers is essential. A service organization or nonprofit organization, by contrast, might measure its success by the number of phone calls it avoids.

Either way, it behooves all organizations to profile and segment their customer bases. Customer profiling begins with an analysis of your customer base. The object is to group, or segment, customers based on their common traits.

To gain an understanding of your customers, you can begin by examining any patterns in their purchases and/or transactions. Next, you can consider which portals your customers use to access your site. Which pages do they view? What paths do they take through your site? To gain a more comprehensive picture of your customers, also take into account psychographic or demographic data (e.g. What kinds of people live in which regions of the country or world?). It is also important to consider the amount of revenue your customer generates. Take into account your organization's cost to acquire and retain each customer and the profit each customer produces. Once you've analyzed this combination of information, you can then begin to segment customers and make predictions about each segment's future behavior and expectations.

In an October 2002 *Line56* article, author David van Everen states the need for customer segmentation. "As companies adopt more customer-centric business processes, service will play a pivotal role in providing personalized interactions. A segmentation strategy that is integrated with customer service provides the framework for delivering an appropriate customer experience based on the customer's value to the organization."

We recommend segmenting your customer base into simple customer tiers based on the relative value each brings to your organization, sometimes referred to as "value-based customer segmentation." It is not unusual for organizations to find that a small portion of high-value customers make up the majority of their profits. It is also not unusual to discover that a small portion of low-value customers may actually cost organizations more than they're worth. Gartner Group's Esteban Kolsky maintains that "about five percent of customers represent 60 percent of revenue for most businesses." He recommends that lower-value customers be directed to self-service phone and Web systems (Hirsh, 2002).

Develop programs to meet your customer's specific needs. Develop offerings which take into consideration your customer's characteristics and your company's ability to provide access to information. Consider offering tiered programs based on a customer's demonstrated skill level, contract type, or product training. For example, the first level of a tiered program may offer customers the opportunity to bypass an initial phone call and log trouble tickets directly into your customer service system or check on the status of an open case. Customers who have completed a training curriculum or who represent a larger contract may be offered a second level program which includes the opportunity to also access the resolution database to search for solutions themselves. A third tier may be developed for your most elite customers, providing them the ability to keep an open dialogue with the knowledge worker assigned to investigate a more elusive problem.

In the illustration below, two customers want to close their accounts. The first tiered customer, or customer level normal, fills out the required paperwork to close his account. The third tier, or platinum level customer, can get the same results by completing an online form. This fictitious organization rewards its most profitable customers with convenience.

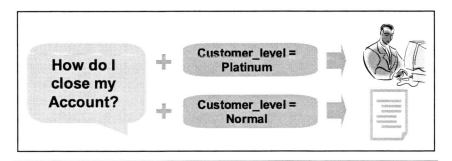

Figure 12.2. Tiered service based on customer value

Offering a variety of programs lets you empower customers at levels which meet their needs and abilities, while providing them with greater customer satisfaction in the solution seeking process. Whenever possible, create an offering which is such a clear opportunity (benefit to cost) that even your least sophisticated customers will want to participate. Finally, encourage exploration and adoption of the new programs by offering them with greater value for the dollar than other programs you would like them to shift from, such as calling a CSR.

When organizations establish effective self-service offerings, service employees are freed up to provide more high-touch, time-consuming attention to the higher value customers. And the beauty of today's technology is that lower-valued customer don't have to be neglected. Organizations can set up sign-in IDs that identify the high-value customers. These IDs can open up or restrict the options customers have access to once they're on your Web site, and they can also establish the order in which e-mail messages are answered. The directive according to Lou Hirsh in a January 7, 2002 CRMDaily article titled, *All Customers are Not Created Equal* is "to do what you can to serve your high-level customers better than your other customers."

Van Everen has a different take on the same subject. He believes that it's not a matter of "the better the customer, the better the service," but rather "for every customer, the appropriate levels of service." His concern is that those companies that strive to differentiate themselves through their service delivery efforts could stand to lose customers and opportunities by catering so one-sidedly to their high-value customers.

Some organizations devote their most experienced service reps to the higher-valued customers. This way, your most valuable customers get what can be assumed to be a higher level of service, but your lower-valued customers' needs also get attention from other service reps. Other organizations may offer the highest tiered customers service benefits such as frequent flier club benefits or credit card points, etc. And, of course, we recommend that the diversion of customer contacts to self-service channels is one effective way to provide all segments of your customer base with good service.

It is important to record the results of your segmentation efforts over time. This way they can be analyzed for effectiveness, and modified, if and when necessary. These records can also be used as justification for additional investment of resources when they show measurable results. Ideally, the practice of customer segmentation will enable organizations to differentiate themselves by offering a unique variety of service to their top tiered customers. At the same time, service standards for remaining customers are not compromised.

External Facing Knowledge Base

The kind of service that creates loyal customers comes down to delivering the right information, to the right person, at the right time. Sounds easy. But as many organizations can attest, this is much more difficult than it sounds. Hewson Consulting was commissioned by eGain to survey United Kingdom organizations that offered Web self-service. His July 2001 article reveals how far organizations have to go to fully leverage Web self-service offerings that create loyal customers. The title and subtitle of the article tells all: "UK Companies Adopt Web Self-Service in Droves, But Fail Miserably in the Quality of Answers. Latest Survey... Reveals 81% of Web sites Offering Self-Help Failed to Deliver Accurate Answers."

In this survey, 140 UK Web sites were surveyed. Thirty-seven percent of the respondents did not offer any form of self-service, super search engine, or FAQ list. Of those that did offer self-service, 58 percent did not make it easy for customers to find these tools online. Amazingly, 100 percent failed to completely answer accurately, and 81 percent failed to even partially answer accurately.

These surveyed organizations and service organizations around the world are discovering that how information is stored, built upon, and organized will determine how effective their service efforts will be. In most service organizations, their primary assets are intellectual. The knowledge worker stands front and center in today's service-oriented economy. The most competitive organizations rely on continual innovation and are committed to investing in the brightest minds.

Rather than depending upon manufacturing plants, machinery, and trucks, the service organizations rely upon intellectual capital. But only when knowledge is shared effectively can it be considered intellectual capital. Thomas Stewart sums up this concept, "Intelligence becomes an asset when useful order is created out of free floating brain power...when it is captured in a way that allows it to be described, shared, and exploited."

In the same way that the Industrial Revolution changed the way businesses operated, the Information Revolution encompasses an equally important and potent shift away from "business as usual." Before the Industrial Revolution, a tradesman or artisan created one product at a time. With the advent of machinery, came the ability to mass produce. Components became standardized and interchangeable; systems became streamlined. So it is in the Information Age. We do not need to design a unique solution for each customer issue. We can store standardized and interchangeable solutions which can be adapted to a variety of customer contacts.

Information abounds, especially since the introduction of the Internet. But that information is useless unless we can make it work for us, unless we can leverage it to create more loyal customers and more productive employees.

While organizations with antiquated data bases could have gotten by years ago, today this is no longer the case. Global competition, employee attrition, organizational and technical complexities, and an ever-expanding amount of incoming and outgoing data drive the need to leverage knowledge. The importance of natural language search engines is to liberate knowledge that may be stuck in less available locations throughout the company's IT infrastructure.

Knowledge Management and Sharing Plan

"Knowledge management" or "information management" are the buzz words. These phrases can be used differently in different organizations. They can include: the strategies and processes of identifying, organizing, and leveraging knowledge, a search engine, an inference engine, document management, the practices necessary to capitalize on the knowledge-based economy, the delivery of just-in-time information, or a discipline that advocates an integrated approach to identifying and sharing the sum of an organization's knowledge assets, including documents, procedures, policies, data bases, and the skills and knowledge of each employee. Knowledge management can be considered the linking of employee's knowledge, skills, expertise, and creations with the technology that organizes and shares this body of information in a strategic way.

As figure 13.1 suggests, when the sum knowledge an organization possesses is not well integrated, your CSRs will have difficulty delivering accurate, timely answers to your customer. This does not serve the customer well. And when the customer is not well served, you can bet he is not loyal to your organization. Everyone loses.

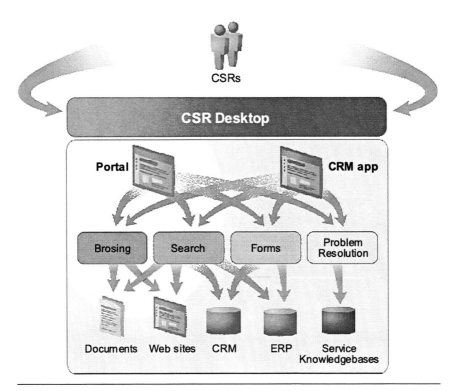

Figure 13.1. First-generation solutions are costly and fail to deliver answers

The core of a knowledge management system is its knowledge base. A knowledge base can be as simple as a library's card catalogue. Information regarding the library's books is organized alphabetically by author, title, and subject. The card catalogue is helpful for those library patrons who come into the library with some knowledge of what they're looking for. In many businesses, the information the customer is looking for is much more complex than a book's title, author's name, or subject. And often, the customer comes to a Web site with little to no knowledge of how to resolve her issue.

Early versions of FAQs are one example of the most basic kind of knowledge base. They were more primitive than even the library card catalogue in that the questions and answers weren't organized in any deliberate order or even cross-referenced. More current FAQs have gotten better. Many are knowledge bases that have cross-referencing capabilities much like the library card catalogue system. Still, these are only rudimentary knowledge bases compared to the higher end knowledge bases that currently exist. More importantly, they are rudimentary when held up against customers' expectations for the right answer at the right time.

Customers' demand for timely, accurate, easy-to-find resolutions means that most businesses must assess their current knowledge bases to ensure they are competitive in today's global economy. Contact center leaders must ask themselves:

- Do we have the staff and systems necessary to keep the knowledge base current? It bears repeating that useless, outdated Web site information can cost you customers. Remember that the competition is only one click away.

- Is our data consistently accurate and complete?

- Are we sure that our Web site's content is driven by customer interest and need? Are we able to reorganize the knowledge base to meet changing customer needs (to accommodate seasonal differences, new product roll outs, etc.)?

- Can we manipulate the list of FAQs easily?

- Is our knowledge base easy to use? Often "ease of use" means that the answers customers seek most frequently are those listed at the top of the FAQ list. Ideally, the answers being sought most often should appear as soon a customer loads the page. If the customer cannot find his answer on our FAQ list, have we provided him with a search option? Is natural language searching available? The natural language search option allows the customer to ask his question in a way that is different from how the information appears on the FAQ; contextual elements of the written language are automatically taken into account by the search engine. Figure 13.2 shows how a natural language search engine works.

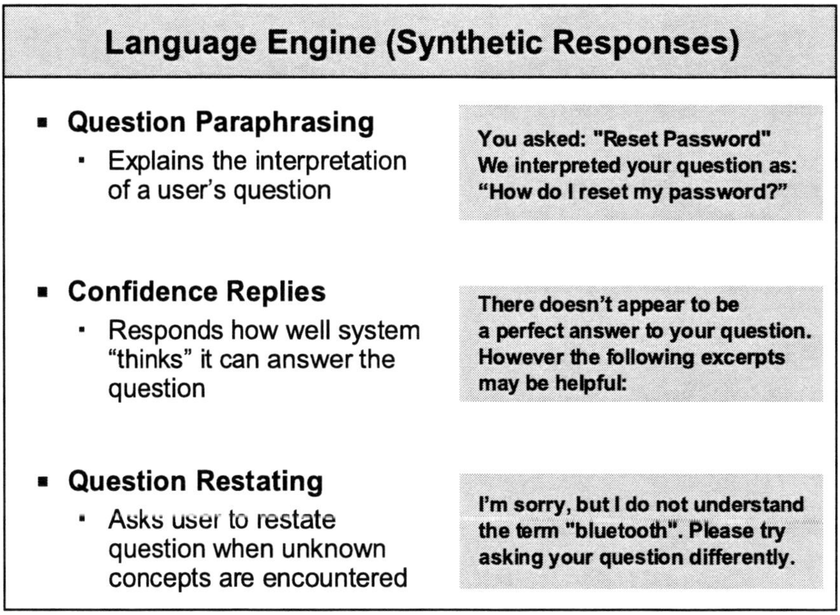

Language Engine (Synthetic Responses)

- **Question Paraphrasing**
  - Explains the interpretation of a user's question

  > You asked: "Reset Password"
  > We interpreted your question as:
  > "How do I reset my password?"

- **Confidence Replies**
  - Responds how well system "thinks" it can answer the question

  > There doesn't appear to be a perfect answer to your question. However the following excerpts may be helpful:

- **Question Restating**
  - Asks user to restate question when unknown concepts are encountered

  > I'm sorry, but I do not understand the term "bluetooth". Please try asking your question differently.

Figure 13.2. Natural language engine

A customer can query, "Reset Password." Even though this isn't the exact phrase listed in your database, a sophisticated engine can still respond effectively to the customer's query with, "We interpreted your question as: 'How do I reset my password?'"

Even when a natural language doesn't make perfect matches between the query and an organization's data base, it can offer a confidence reply such as, "There doesn't appear to be a perfect answer to your question. However, the following excerpts may be helpful..." And even when a customer poses a question the search engine doesn't recognize, it can respond intelligently with an answer such as, "I'm sorry, but I do not understand the term 'bluetooth.' Please try asking your question differently."

- Do we give our customers the option of contacting a CSR if they are not able to find the resolution they seek?
- Do our customers' questions and corresponding answers automatically get added to our knowledge base so that it can help future customers? (Warner, 2000: paraphrased text)

Transformation of Data into Actionable Knowledge

Well designed Internet customer service knowledge bases automate much of the work it takes to deliver those right answers to the right person at the right time. Some organizations choose to seed their knowledge base initially with a list of FAQs. After that initial seeding, all FAQs in the knowledge base are entered, sorted, and interrelated based on customer input. The site's administrator only needs to interact with the knowledge base when a customer asks a question that hasn't been asked or answered before.

Your knowledge base content will ideally be driven by your customers. Often, customers will provide feedback regarding their online experience. By acting upon this feedback, you will not only improve the customer's experience but you will also reduce the work load of your employees. The more useful the site, the more likely you are to steer customers away from needing help from a service rep.

Knowledge Gathered from Explicit and Tacit Sources

Your customers' feedback can come from explicit as well as tacit sources (tacit means deduced from watching customer behavior). Explicit customer feedback can come in the form of a customer's feedback or question regarding a single FAQ or a group of FAQs. A customer's direct question to a service rep and a customer-completed survey are other forms of explicit feedback that can be used to tailor your site's content.

We recommend that when it comes to ordering your site's FAQs that you leverage information from tacit sources as well. The tacit rankings are collected by analyzing the paths your customers take through your Web site. This click-stream analysis helps organizations understand the effectiveness of their site's content and other communication channels. It also helps organizations better understand their customers and how they interface with the organization.

This information is a feature typically available with most vendors' technology.

The beauty of knowledge management is its versatility of uses. The same knowledge base that improves service to your customers can be used by new CSRs as an information resource. Leveraged fully, this resource can function as a learning tool to help your new reps become more productive more quickly.

Internal Facing Knowledge Base

Internal facing knowledge bases benefit your employee group even more directly. They facilitate easier access to information the employees need to do their jobs. Instead of being inundated with more information and more paper than they can handle, internal facing knowledge bases help employees sift out what is useful and relevant. The employee saves time digging for information and his productivity improves.

Also, instead of allowing decades worth of knowledge and experience walk out the door with each retiree (or promotions and attrition), internal facing knowledge bases have tapped into and captured that information. Ideally, the expert's tacit knowledge can remain within the organization even after the expert has left.

Effective knowledge bases can also help organizations prevent the continual reinvention of the wheel. When knowledge is captured and stored over time, employees can look at existing processes, documents, and the like, examine them, and improve upon them. The organization benefits by reducing the likelihood of second and third iterations of the wheel. Leveraging organizational knowledge is essential for those organizations who want to flourish in today's world economy.

As you approach the improvement of your current knowledge base, keep in mind the following:

- Experts warn that 30 to 50 percent of the information in a typical database is missing or inaccurate.

- Understand the interrelationships between the databases that currently exist in your organization. These interrelationships must be maintained through any conversion.

- Recognize equivalent entities and heterogeneous systems. One important piece of information may appear under different field names in different parts of your organization. (Two groups might be serving the same customer but have entered the name differently; one database lists Castaneda Dunham, Inc., and the other CDI.)

- As soon as you're able, create and capture metadata for interfaces, business processes, and database requirements (metadata and meta-analysis is a statistical integration of data accumulated across many different studies). You will need to synchronize the metadata between different functions, different metadata stores, and different vendor products.

- When selecting data transformation tools, look for tools that make it possible to map data from source to target with a simple point-and-click interface. Also try to find a tool that can capture and store metadata during the conversion process.

- Take advantage of external information sources. For example, you may be able to obtain a database that contains the average income for every ZIP code in the country. This could help you segment all 20–30 year olds in a specific region for an upcoming targeted marketing campaign.

- The hardware requirements for data warehousing database servers is significant. Many CPU cycles are required to slice and dice data repetitively to meet the different needs of users throughout your organization. It is wise to select a scalable platform no matter how much headroom you've provided in your server specification.

- The average cost to build a data warehouse is $1.8 million.

Currently multi-channel contact centers abound. The good news is the potential cost savings to organizations and the increased customer choice that these centers offer. The bad news, or "challenges" as some optimists would say, are described in a recent TMCnet.com article. Writer Laurent Philonenko explains, "Successfully managing and fulfilling each customer transaction, regardless of media channel, is likely to be the greatest challenge contact centers will face over the next two years. Examples abound of multi-channel deployments, but today they are usually disjointed...It is important to note that the provision and support of multimedia customer service through a universal queue and the ability to capture and benefit from customer information across all channels are the most urgent needs to be addressed by contact centers today." (Philonenko, 2002)

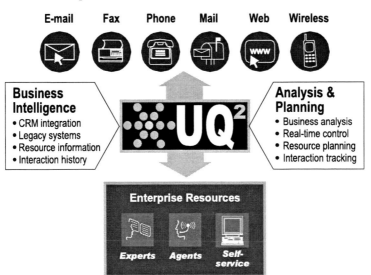

Multi-Channel, Value-Based CRM Requires a Universal Queue

E-mail   Fax   Phone   Mail   Web   Wireless

Business Intelligence
• CRM integration
• Legacy systems
• Resource information
• Interaction history

UQ²

Analysis & Planning
• Business analysis
• Real-time control
• Resource planning
• Interaction tracking

Enterprise Resources

Experts   Agents   Self-service

Figure 14.1. The Genesys universal queue

Call centers that haven't strategically planned their evolution into contact centers typically make the mistake of having a separate queue for each media type. The main focus typically is on the phone call queue. Alternative channels may have been developed and managed by separate organizations, each utilizing separate databases, and each using different metrics. What results is the inefficient use of call center and technology resources. More importantly, customers will likely notice an inconsistent service experience across the different types of media.

Ideally, contact centers will use a common management structure, common workgroups, common business rules, and integrated databases for customer contact history and reporting. Consistency in service results are the byproduct, not of haphazard initiatives but, of clear strategic planning, collaboration, and a common set of metrics.

At the core of the integrated contact center is the universal queue. It is a virtual waiting line for all customer contacts, no matter which channel the customer chooses. By centralizing these contacts, they can be analyzed, routed, and documented by the same software solutions. Because each solution is subjected to similar processing logic, customers are offered a consistent level of service.

The universal queue also allows for skills-based routing strategies to be utilized. This ensures that only an agent with the appropriate knowledge and skills responds to the customer. A customer who requests a chat session would be routed to an agent with strong writing skills.

Priority routing allows contact center leadership the ability to prioritize customer contacts based on media type. Depending on customer needs and business considerations, a phone call may be given higher priority, for example, than an e-mail request for information.

One of the advantages of the integrated contact center is that customer contact histories are centralized. A single historical record stores all interactions between a customer and the contact center, regardless of what communication channel the customer used.

In a CRMDaily DotCom special report titled, *Meeting the Multichannel Service Challenge*, Gartner Group vice president Michael Moaz lifts up clothing retailer Talbots as an organization that is meeting this challenge. Moaz attributes Talbots' success to the fact that the organization organizes all contact channels under a single management structure and workflow. Moaz says that, "If you interact with a contact center agent via Talbots on the Web, he or she is the same person you would call with a catalog order, either from your home phone or in the store. Their goal is brand reinforcement, and the channels are not separate areas. Thus, they have higher than industry-average sales." (Hill, 2002)

Philonenko sums up the challenge that faces contact center leadership, "The option of implementing point solutions in the contact center and hoping for the best is definitely over. It may be easier action to take than re-engineering the way in which you do business, but leading companies around the world are planning their communication and knowledge sharing strategies for the next 10 years. Those that do not will lose customers, revenue, and profitability."

CHAPTER 15: CREATING VALUE WITH NATURAL LANGUAGE SEARCH

Acknowledgement

This chapter is a slightly revised paper written by David Daniels of Jupiter Media. Details and questions can be directed to <ddaniels@jupitermedia.com>. The treatise was selected for reproduction here with the approval of the author because it so closely reflects and validates the opinions and findings of the authors.

Too often, a Web site searchable self-service is simply not useful to customers. Most searches generate pages and pages of unfocused results that offer little more value than an FAQ would. By implementing natural language (NL) search functionality, sites can provide the efficient online self-service consumers seek, while collecting valuable usage data about the customer.

Key Questions

1. How is the online self-service experience affecting consumer attitudes?

2. What role can natural language search play in customer support?

3. What are the organizational, operational, and technical steps to improving the usefulness of searchable self-service? What are the key performance indicators and measures of success?

Key Takeaways

1. Fifty-four percent of consumers who had difficulties related to the usability of online customer service said self-service search returns too many results to be useful.

2. Corporate spending on self-service search and knowledge management applications will double over the next four years, reaching $2.8 billion in 2007.

3. Implementing self-service search to deflect customer service contacts is shortsighted; poor implementations can lead to customer defection and increased contact volume.

4. Companies must use reciprocal interaction (i.e., using search algorithms to propel customers into a one-on-one dialogue with a company, via e-mail, chat, or other method). Natural language search provides the best opportunity for companies to understand customer inflection points—not contact deflection points.

5. Businesses must use natural language search to improve the user experience and effectiveness of search result pages, crafting pages that deliver one or two relevant content assets to direct consumers to a desired task.

6. Self-help does not equal customer service. At best, natural language search is an analog to CSR interaction and should be used to triage basic customer queries.

7. While self-service search can lower contact volumes, the net effect on staffing is simply to delay new hiring rather than affect a wholesale agent workforce reduction.

Consumers Frustrated with Online Self-service Search

Companies are preoccupied with self-service to gain efficiency within the service organization, yet consumers fail to find such efficiency in their self-service searches. Self-service search is plagued with usability issues; 54 percent of consumers who report usability issues said searches offer too many results to be effective.

Despite Popularity, Searchable Self-service Suffers from Low Usage

The question asked was "Thinking about the last time you contacted customer service on a shopping site, which service method did you use first? (Select one)" (Jupiter, 2002)

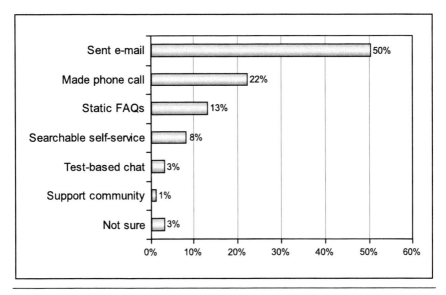

Figure 15.1. Online customer service method consumers used first during latest contact

While consumers still rely on search as an alternative means of Web site navigation, search is hardly on consumers' minds when they seek customer support (see *Web Site Search: Understanding and Influencing Customer Behavior*, Site Technologies & Operations, February 4, 2003). Although 80 percent of consumers Jupiter surveyed said they have used searchable self-service during the past six months, just eight percent said it was the first support option they used for their most recent inquiry. As consumers look for a gratifying and efficient online service experience, many opt for asynchronous communications channels (e.g., e-mail), due in part to the low number of self-service systems deployed. A December 2002 Jupiter WebTrack found searchable self-service deployed on 18 percent of the 227 sites sampled.

Searchable Self-service Can Play a Role in Retention and Acquisition

The convenience of online self-service affects consumers' selection of which sites to do business with: 25 percent of online buyers Jupiter surveyed said the existence of self-service search would determine which sites they would make future purchases from. The attitude that drives do-it-yourself behavior is borne from a desire for convenience. Ultimately, self-service frees consumers from having to wait for an answer to a query. Yet, such convenience has hardly been realized; searchable service options continue to frustrate online consumers.

Convenience of Self-service Search Marred by Usability Issues

The question asked was, "Please select the following options that best describe your attitude and behavior related to searchable self-service on Web sites (i.e., the ability to search for answers to a question by typing in a phrase or full sentence in a search box). (Select all that apply.)" (Jupiter, 2002)

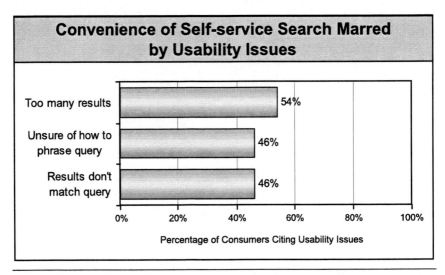

Figure 15.2. Online customer service usability issues consumers cited

It is ironic that although companies have been preoccupied with implementing searchable self-service to increase efficiency within service organizations, many consumers view such offerings as a waste of time. Consumer attitudes point to a failure among sites to provide a consistent and gratifying experience via search. Analysis of survey data among consumers who cited self-service usability issues yielded the following conclusions:

Results pages provide little more benefit than static FAQ lists. Fifty-four percent of these consumers said self-service search simply returns too many results to be useful. Regardless of whether a search is executed through a keyword or natural language query, simply returning a list of links has failed to improve the effectiveness of online self-service.

Little consistency among search fields impedes experience. Forty-six percent of such consumers said they are unsure of how to phrase their search questions to get the best results. Although sites could easily address the situation by providing better guidance, the historical prevalence of keyword search is undermining the use of natural language queries.

Resulting content does not satisfy customer intent. Forty-six percent said self-service results do not answer their queries, indicating that common keyword search deployments have done little to measure customer intent and signaling organizations' failure to calibrate and maintain content to meet customers' needs.

Illogical separation of site and self-service search further complicates usability. Common site search tools are not being applied to online self-help resources. When testing banking sites that have both site search and self-service search functions, Jupiter could only find one example in which a site search returned the customer service content accessible through searchable self-service.

Call Deflection Can Drive Customer Defection

Jupiter has documented the adverse impact that poor customer service (self-service included) has on customer retention (Jupiter, 2003). Moreover, a poor self-service implementation can actually increase the number of service contacts a company must handle. In a survey Bank of America fielded to its customers in July 2002, of people who were dissatisfied with their search results, 60 percent said they would make a phone call, and 23 percent said they would send an e-mail message to get further information. This echoes Jupiter's findings that poor online service will drive customers to the phone, ultimately minimizing any benefits derived from online self-service.

Mass Adoption of Online Self-service Limited by Inconsistent User Experience

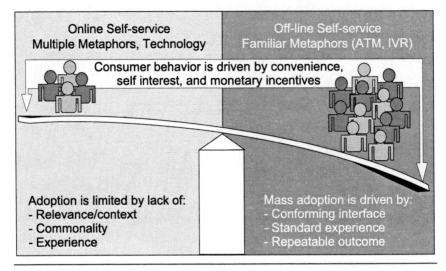

Figure 15.3. Limitations of online self-service (Jupiter, 2003)

Organizations' desire to quash support costs using self-service search has led them to apply self-service systems far too broadly. Online self-service has been poisoned by the universal lack of consistent, repeatable outcomes. The lack of a consistent user experience (i.e., nonconforming) is one of the greatest inhibitors to self-service search adoption. While many companies use the Pareto Principle (i.e., the 80/20 rule) to allocate support resources and content to customer inquiries, most do not realize that this rule does not apply to the totality of the consumer online self-service experience. That is, from site to site or among a company's own sites, no common experience accounts for 80 percent of consumers' self-service search usage. While search boxes are familiar to users, the subsequent results pages lack conformity or predictability. Success of self-service off-line (e.g., ATMs) is due in part to conforming interfaces that deliver a consistent experience and repeatable outcome.

Self-service Search Vendors to Consolidate on NL, Capture Two-fold Spending Increase

Spending on self-service search and knowledge management applications will double over the next four years, reaching $2.8 billion in 2007. Vendors will consolidate around natural language (NL) search, as leaders will shift the market's focus away from returning lists of search results to presenting a much richer environment, delivering consumers to a single relevant result or task.

Self-service Search Spending to Increase in Coming Two to Three Years

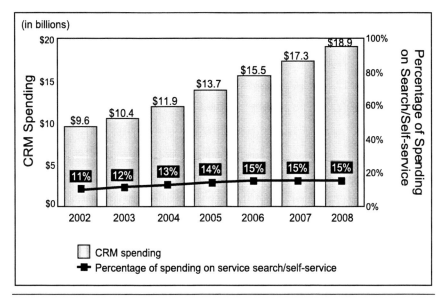

Figure 15.4. CRM spending, as percentage of self-service spending, 2002–2008 (Jupiter, 2002)

Spending on self-service search and searchable knowledge management applications will increase from $1.1 billion in 2002 to $2.8 billion in 2007, ultimately accounting for 15 percent of CRM application spending in the US. This increase is driven by the desire among companies to deflect inquiries from support staff. Fifty-three percent of executives Jupiter surveyed in November 2002 said they planned to implement searchable self-service in the next six to 12 months, while only 18 percent had such systems in place at the time, as revealed in a December 2002 WebTrack. Over time, searchable knowledge-retrieval applications will become the major operational CRM investment because companies perceive it to be a cost-effective means to reduce support expenditures.

Web Services to Keep Deployment Costs Relatively Flat

Compared with other CRM suite components, such as CSR desktop applications, searchable self-service solutions are relatively affordable. Downward price pressure on servers will keep deployment costs relatively flat, not exceeding $150,000, on average. Additionally, the pricing plateau will be driven, in part, by the introduction of data exchange standards in the form of Web services, which will eradicate the need for search and knowledge management providers to rely on keyword meta-tags and sell custom application interfaces, data conduits, and platform-specific knowledge repositories.

Vendors Rally Around NL Search; Interface and Data Access Flexibility Drive Success

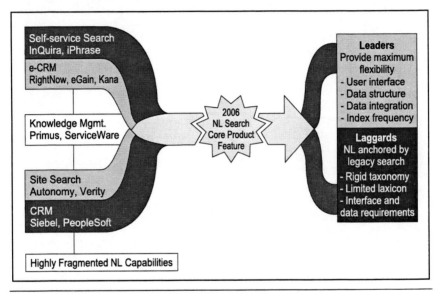

Figure 15.5. Self-service vendor evolution (Jupiter, 2003)

Vendors across several categories (e.g., knowledge management, site search, and CRM), chasing the billions of dollars spent on self-service search, will strive to be recognized for a compelling solution. Enterprise CRM vendors have entered into OEM licensing agreements to bolster the natural language (NL) processing capabilities of their products, while others have acquired NL technology companies. Through the ability to support rich NL queries, two categories will classify self-service search vendors over the next 24 months:

NL processing. These vendors that offer NL technology as a means to process queries and return a familiar search results page.

114

Contextual experience management. In addition to using NL, conceptual, and semantic linguistics, these vendors will deliver enriched search results. Similar to personalization in content management systems, they will harness the power of NL processing and tie it to business rules, promoting reciprocal interaction so results pages are formatted differently based on the query, user profile, and previous behavior.

Jupiter Concept: Reciprocal Interaction

Reciprocal interaction involves using linguistic, conceptual, and semantic processing of search queries, as well as business rules, to propel customers into a dialogue with a company (e.g., via e-mail, chat, or voice). Rather than deflecting customer contacts toward Web pages that answer queries using text or graphics, this notion embraces contact with customers.

Market Leaders Will Provide Maximum Flexibility in Indexing, Presentation, and Integration

As the searchable self-service landscape continues to shift, vendors with the following characteristics will emerge as leaders:

Flexible user interface and presentation options. Successful vendors will focus on usability, offering a variety of interface options, such as "conversational bots." Moreover, leaders will provide the capability to orient search results in every possible manner, transcending style sheet-driven templates to provide an experience that defines a site, whether in a JSP, Flash MX, or HTML template environment.

Ability to yield a variety of data sources and types. Laggards will continue to promote only structured search, largely driven by single keywords, metadata, or question-and-answer pairs trapped in their own frameworks. They will also continue to advocate the replication of assets in a proprietary environment. Leaders will present the same results, as well as information within unstructured documents and data from other IT systems (e.g., transactional account information).

Variable and real-time indexing capabilities. Leading solutions will offer variable intervals at which assets can be indexed—over the conventional approach of one-off indexing. This will allow the inclusion of fluid data such as account information and transactions to surface, as well as incorporate frequent changes to support documents.

Contextual experience management. Leading vendors will carve out a new category of personalization not only driven by personas or profiles, but also the context of consumers' behavior, taking into account attitudinal nuances of a query. Results will be nuggets of content as well as interactive customer service escalation options including e-mail, text chat, and voice. These vendors will transform the self-service search experience by injecting users into relevant tasks.

Universal Action Plan: Use Self-service Search to Invite Dialogue; Set Realistic Success Measures

The true opportunity of natural language search is to foster reciprocal interaction and understanding of customers' inflection points, not deflection points. At best, self-service search delays service staffing needs by 12 to 18 months. Companies must not expect a wholesale labor reduction; instead, they must absorb short-term workforce gains by reallocating staff to customer retention activities.

Strategy

Self-help Benefits Short-circuited by Persistent Contact Volume Growth

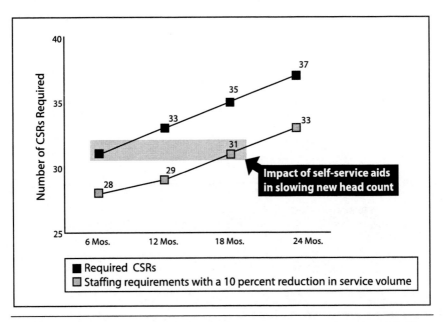

Figure 15.6. Impact of Rising Contact Center Volume Benefit of Self-service

116

Note: Assumes base of 29 FTEs, starting with 40,000 inbound inquiries per month. Factors three percent growth in service volume monthly (Jupiter, 2002).

Companies have been fooled into thinking self-help means "customer service." It does not. While self-service solutions are an excellent tactic to handle basic questions, their impact will only slow the rising tide of service contacts, not eradicate all contacts. While NL queries simulate a dialogue between customer and company, they must be viewed as a triage layer that helps liberate staff from mundane requests.

Labor Reductions Should Not Be Goal of Self-service

Impact on Inquiry Volume from Self-service	
Reduction in Inquiry Volume	**Impact on Staffing†**
5 percent	Consistent for 11 months, 3 new hires required in 12th month
10 percent	Consistent for 17 months, 3 new hires required in 18th month
15 percent	Reduces staff by 3 for first 18 months, 3 new hires needed in 24th month

†Factors three percent growth in contact volume monthly (Jupiter, 2003).

Jupiter projects online service contacts will grow at a combined annual growth rate (CAGR) of 28 percent over the next 12 months. Given this growth, a successful self-service search solution will likely delay the hiring of additional service staff, not reduce headcount. Jupiter's contact reduction model indicates a three percent rise in service volume per month. (For details on the contact reduction model, Jupiter clients can view a spreadsheet alongside this report on <www.jup.com>.) Using a baseline of 29 full-time equivalent (FTE) staff, handling 40,000 inbound contacts per month, the model implies three percent growth in contact volume per month. The scenarios indicated in Figure 15.7 are based on contact reductions attributable to the introduction of self-service search (Jupiter, 2003).

While a relatively dramatic reduction in inquiry volume of 15 percent would result in three fewer service staff needed during the first 12 months, businesses must realize the benefits are short-lived; trimming head count will lead to higher costs later, given an average of $8,000 needed to hire and train a new CSR.

The goal of implementing self-service automation must be to liberate service staff from fielding mundane requests and tasks, allowing them to concentrate on delivering consistently excellent service to valued customers and devoting more time to retention-oriented activities such as customer outreach.

Execution

Use NL Search to Create Contextually Relevant Navigation

Like keyword search, natural language (NL) search (e.g., phrasing a query in the form of a question) is based on a conforming user-input template (i.e., universal search field), but a valuable difference is the way a query can be parsed to present an enriched experience that injects a user into a task. For example, searching on "How do I reorder checks?" would bring a user to the actual order page, not a description page with a link; an experience keyword matching cannot accomplish easily.

NL search is well suited to alleviate consumers' frustrations: It makes search more efficient in addressing queries with relevant content, and provides contextually relevant navigation, a task-oriented experience that guides a user to a desired outcome. While it is possible to deliver such dynamic navigation using keyword tags at little to no additional technology investment, it does require significant manual oversight. Using NL search to process queries and guide business rules that present this enriched user experience is a best practice.

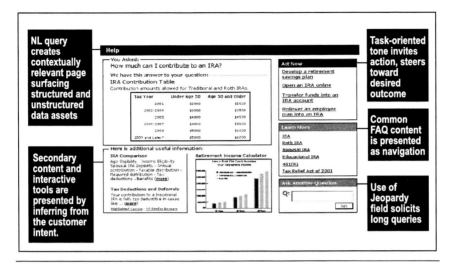

Figure 15.7. NL search best practice example (Jupiter, 2003)

Deliver Single Complete Pages, Not Laundry List of Links

Businesses must use NL search to craft results pages that deliver one or two relevant content assets to inject a consumer into a desired task. While a self-service solution's ability to aggregate a variety of structured and unstructured content is crucial, companies must pay close attention to the usability and subsequent experience of search results. The following are NL search best practices:

1. Solicit NL queries via a "Jeopardy Field." Use a long-form search field and direct users to issue search queries as a question. Labels used by BellSouth and GE Appliance, such as "Ask (brand name)" or "Ask Customer Support" have worked well to solicit longer queries that more accurately reflect consumers' intent.

2. Provide most often asked questions as examples of search string form. Doing so provides an expression of the desired user input while offering the most common questions asked. A top nationwide long distance provider realized an 80 percent drop in service-related e-mail messages within two weeks of adopting this approach.

3. Place NL searches in front of e-mail contact forms. Harness content reserved for feeding e-mail responses and expose it externally. BellSouth posted the top five most frequently

119

asked questions above its e-mail contact form, reducing e-mail volume by 10 to 30 percent based on the topic. Other companies, such as Thule, a manufacturer of auto utility racks, and BEA, have taken a more integrated approach, pushing e-mail submissions through a knowledge base, from which possible answers are returned. Such tactics have reduced e-mail volume in some cases by between two and three percent.

4. Use reciprocal interaction. NL search is an efficient means to propel customers to an e-mail, text chat, or voice interaction, as appropriate. Queries can be given an attitudinal score based on their words and tone, allowing customers to be escalated to a real-time contact if needed. In the absence of attitudinal routing, companies must present contact options for when a query fails to deliver results. BellSouth invites search users into a text chat session if content doesn't match a query or if a visitor's session goes over a specified period of time—which, as BellSouth has found, signals a high level of frustration.

5. Use static FAQs on side navigation to bring customers to related content and tasks. Harness the abundance of static FAQs by presenting them as related content. Companies can disguise such content as navigation by using task-oriented labels such as "reorder checks" or "reset password," taking users to a desired task rather than a piece of content that explains how to complete the task.

6. Allow site search to access self-service search. Allow keyword searches from site search forms to be applied to the NL search engine. Fidelity Investments, for example, allows input in its small keyword site search box to be processed by an NL search engine.

Develop Usability Scenarios to Manage Customer Inflection Points

NL processing excels at uncovering the nuances of customers' intent. Analytics inherent in NL applications provide companies with useful customer metrics that can guide the management of customer relationships both online and off-line. LPL Financial, for example, marries its NL search logs to its brokerages profiles, and its management team reaches out to brokers when usage and training implications are identified. To maximize the impact these measures will have, companies must create persona-based scenarios prior to a self-service deployment. Such scenarios should identify desired outcomes and customer behavior, for example, determining which search strings will be met with content and which provide an opportunity for interaction or revenue. Simply defining contact deflection as a customer experience goal is not enough. The real opportunity exists in understanding customer inflection points, not deflection points. A deployment archetype should account for the benefits of NL search, such as the ability to define the experience through customers' intent.

Address Organizational Deficits Prior to Technology Selection

To maximize the success of a self-service offering, companies must address the following knowledge management principles before seeking a self-service search provider:

Calibration. Ensure the necessity, structure, and relevance of knowledge assets with a knowledge task force. Over two to four weeks, interview service staff and customers in order to ensure the most relevant service content is acquired and accurate. Analyze existing search logs to determine likely topics. Identify sources of content while understanding the implications of content's structure, source, and creation process.

Responsibility. Clearly understand the governance and workload requirements of managing knowledge assets on an ongoing basis. Jupiter's executive interviews found several examples of staff requirements needed after an NL search solution had been deployed; accordingly, companies must commit at least one-half or a full FTE to the care and feeding of the solution. Identify an individual capable of acting as a liaison across all content sources, as well as someone well versed in measurement. Much of the post-deployment effort will center on filling content holes and crafting new experiences to match customer intent better.

121

Quantify Empirical Benefits of Self-service to Measure Success

Success Metrics			
External-Customer and Technology		**Internal-Business and Technology**	
Measure	**Matrix, Proxy Attributes**	**Measure**	**Matrix, Proxy Attributes**
Customer satisfaction	Self-service adoption rate	Support costs	Incident creation rate, service volume growth
Results yield	Task completion click-through rate	Support quality	Customer satisfaction, CSR quality scores
Experience	Adoption, traffic influence metrics	Customer intent	Business, site and product improvements

Figure 15.8. Suggested success metrics for online self-service (Jupiter, 2003)

Considering market dynamics, as well as internal and external forces that contribute to service volume, the benefits of deploying self-service are hard to measure. Companies should adopt the following measurements that, in aggregate, represent a proxy for the deployment's success.

1. **Incident creation rate**. This measurement compares the number of e-mail inquiries received at the contact center with the number of self-service search sessions initiated. While results vary by industry, target an average creation rate of 70 percent. Thule has achieved a creation rate of roughly 55 percent using RightNow's solution.

2. **Service volume growth rate**. Measured across voice and e-mail touch points, service volume and subsequent staff growth rates should be monitored to gauge the solutions' impact on hiring requirements. For example, BEA's support staff had been increasing 11 percent per month, but since deploying InQuira's solution, growth slowed to three percent

per month, which BEA estimates totals $3 million in annual savings.

3. **Self-service adoption**. Adoption can be skewed by a number of factors including the prominence of the solution across a site. However, companies such as BellSouth have seen a 60 percent year-over-year growth in the number of self-service sessions. This, coupled with service volume growth rate, will gauge a solution's ability to change customer behavior and act as a proxy for the self-service experience.

4. **Satisfaction**. Although companies such as Gateway have achieved a 30 percent increase in customer satisfaction, companies should target a 10 percent increase in customer satisfaction conservatively and at least a five percent improvement on internal quality measures.

5. **Results yield**. Also a proxy for a measure of a customer's site experience, look for increases in success metrics (i.e., conversion) and click-through from self-service content to measure improvements in task completion.

6. **Customer intent**. Measure the occurrences when NL learnings have led to a product or site improvement. The goal should not be to increase the number of self-service solutions, but rather to measure customer intent more accurately to improve site usability and off-line support tools (e.g., product manuals) and reduce overall service inquiries—including self-service sessions. Every company Jupiter interviewed encountered business improvements that were an outgrowth of measuring customer intent, including: improving site usability (Bank of America added and improved access to online banking center and ATM locators), identifying product demand (Thule identified increased demand for "downhill bike" racks), and improving product support materials (BEA and Kensington improved product documentation and CSR training).

BellSouth Measures Customer Intent, Reduces E-mail Volume with NL Search—a case study

Participants:

BellSouth, a Fortune 100 telecommunications company, operates Bellsouth.com to support its business and residential customers. Founded in 1997, Broad Daylight offers both hosted and licensed on-premises versions of natural language (NL) self-service search product, BroadMind.

Goals:

BellSouth, not satisfied with the customer experience of its site, sought to replace its keyword search engine. It wanted to replace static FAQs and the administration associated with updating such content. Additionally, BellSouth aimed to improve search satisfaction across the site, as well as use NL search to affect cost savings.

Execution:

After extensive vendor evaluations, BellSouth deployed the hosted version of Broad Daylight's BroadMind product in January 2002. The company trialed the system in its contact center for three months to test the knowledge management solution for accuracy and performance. Initially accessible only through the customer service section of bellsouth.com, the application was later implemented throughout the site in areas additional customer assistance is most often needed, such as account provisioning.

Economics:

After contracting with Broad Daylight, the solution took roughly two months to deploy. BellSouth dedicated one full-time staff member to manage the solution, which included crafting content, monitoring usage, and driving increased results performance. Based on previous Broad Daylight deployments Jupiter estimates the solution and its implementation cost roughly $150,000 to $200,000. BellSouth executives have been thrilled with the system, which has slowed the rate at which the company hires new service center staff, and has liberated CSRs from mundane tasks to do customer outreach via text chat. Additionally, by placing "Ask BellSouth" above an e-mail contact form, BellSouth has reduced its e-mail volume by 10 to 30 percent, based on the topic. For example, on common inquiries such as "forgetting log-in names and passwords," the company has seen even more dramatic decreases. BellSouth has also seen a rapid increase in the ability to deploy site enhancements, noting the "speed to measure customer intent and implement improvements based on customer feedback is very compressed." Jupiter estimates that by virtue of fewer e-mail and off-line contacts BellSouth receives, and the associated delay in new hiring, the implementation of Broad Daylight has, at the very least, paid for itself.

Bottom Line:

BellSouth has used NL search universally to measure customer intent and react to customer feedback accordingly. As advocated by Jupiter in this report, the company has reinvested the efficiency gains that e-mail volume reductions have afforded it by assigning CSRs to customer outreach, automatically involving CSRs in customer Web site sessions when search strings fail or when session lengths go beyond a prescribed period of time, all in the name of improving customer service.

Bank of America Finds Value in NL Self-service Search—a case study

Participants:

With 4,400 domestic offices and 13,000 ATMs nationwide, Bank of America operates a Web site that provides online banking access to more than 4.7 million active users. InQuira, formed from the merger of Electric Knowledge and Answerfriend, developed an natural language (NL) search solution aimed at external self-service. The solution is also offered for internal contact center search functions and knowledge retrieval purposes.

Goals:

Bank of America sought to improve its site and self-service search to provide a highly functional online channel where customers can manage their finances easily and securely. The company's aim was to improve customers' experience, while moving basic service requests to the Web site, and increase the number of online banking clients, which it has found are more profitable than off-line-only clients.

Execution:

After a vendor "bake-off" in late 2000, the InQuira solution was deployed in early 2001. Bank of America executives said they selected the solution because of its cost-effectiveness in supporting the idiosyncrasies of its site and that it did not require a site redesign. Initially accessible only through an "Ask a Question" link in the site's global "Help" navigation, the system was extended to the entire site in 2002.

Economics:

After contracting with InQuira, it took five months to deploy the solution. The Bank of America installation included procurement and installation of new hardware, which added approximately two months to the schedule. Beyond the initial seeding of the most common question-and-answer pairs, the solution required very little content administration, which Jupiter estimates to be less than one full-time equivalent (FTE) staff member, amounting to no more than $10,000 in direct staffing costs. Based on other InQuira deployments, Jupiter estimates that the solution and its implementation cost roughly $150,000 to $200,000. While return on investment is difficult to quantify, the system has increased self-service sessions and, more important, lead to a number of site improvements that have better defined the site experience, which the company believes has driven additional online banking usage.

Bottom Line:

As Jupiter advocates, Bank of America has found the real benefit of searchable service to be improved ability to measure customer intent and turn such insight into business benefits. NL search vastly improved Bank of America's ability to measure customer intent; the "Ask a Question" search strings have totaled 6.3 words in length, while the previous keyword-oriented search only garnered 2.2 words. This knowledge allowed the company to change the site to meet customers' needs and led to the introduction or improvement of many self-service applications (e.g., locators, and password/PIN functions). Bank of America executives agree with Jupiter's position. One commented, "while we believe that it has resulted in call/contact deflection, it has been difficult to track contact pattern at the user level," adding that the true benefit has been "understanding visitor language and changing the user's interface to satisfy a need."

Definitions

CRM Spending

Jupiter defines CRM spending as the hardware and software costs associated with deployment of customer service systems.

Current Market Size

Jupiter estimates that companies spent $9.6 billion on CRM operations in 2002, up slightly from $9.5 million in 2001. To assess current market size, Jupiter used the following sources:

- Executive surveys of companies employing CRM initiatives
- Executive interviews with leading companies in the CRM space
- Public financial filings of leading companies in the CRM space

In summary, we have made a strong case for the following recommendations for implementing a Web-based self-service channel:

- Give customers choices when it comes to which channel they wish to be serviced through. What's best for the customer will often be best for the company.

- Offer self-service, but do not make it the only channel. Learn from the experiences banks had with the ATM, and that airlines are currently encountering with the ticketing kiosk. Give customer choices. Let customers decide what is best for them and they will be much happier.

- Make sure that your self-service channel is enabled with a powerful natural language search engine that literally interprets the customer's questions and is intuitive enough to add rich content to the accurate answer.

- Make sure that your self-service channel is seamlessly and intuitively connected to the chat, e-mail, and ultimately the telephone channel.

In conclusion, we have shown you that:

- Customers quickly adopt Web-based self-service for simple transactions that save them time and potentially money.

- Web-based self-service can substantially reduce the cost of live calls and reduce agent attrition by removing many, if not all, low value and boring questions.

- Web-based self-service is the obvious answer to the ever-increasing demand of customers for access to mission-critical information related to the use of products and services.

- And finally, that Web-based self-service that is good for the customer is also good for the customer service knowledge worker.

Background

Today's business environment demands that companies thoughtfully consider technology investments with the bottom line in mind. However, with new technologies come new business processes that can challenge a company's understanding of the financial impact. InQuira 6 represents one of these new technologies. InQuira 6 is a customer search and navigation application used by companies to optimize the Web experience of their prospects and customers. It enables Web site visitors to ask a question in natural language, and then interprets the real intent of their query, responding with the precise answer and enriching the response by guiding the user to contextually-related content including opportunities to buy products and services.

> ### A New Standard for Web Self-Service ROI
>
> *The traditional approach to quantifying the ROI for Web self-service is to look at call center deflection. While useful and compelling, new applications like InQuira 6 provide additional functionality that sets a higher standard and broadens the ROI impact to pre-sales marketing efforts.*
>
> *InQuira 6 gives marketers:*
>
> - Business rules. Advanced business rules in InQuira 6 give marketing managers unprecedented control over precise content returned to users from a query, including the ability to introduce cross-sell and up-sell merchandising opportunities.
>
> - Dynamic Navigation User Interface (UI). InQuira 6's User Interface is made up of components that allow marketing managers to provide customers with additional content relevant to their queries.
>
> - Customer insight. Analytics packaged with InQuira 6 gives online marketers and customer service professionals deep insight into customers' online behavior, enabling businesses the power to continually assess and improve the quality of their customers' online experience.

The purpose of this paper is to outline a model that companies can use to understand the potential ROI (Return On Investment) of InQuira applications. The simple models that most self service search companies use revolve around cost-savings from phone call and e-mail deflection. However, InQuira 6 ships with functionality that improves the pre-sales marketing and selling capabilities as well, making the ROI case stronger. This model, therefore, looks both at the traditional cost-savings a company can expect, as well as the potential revenue that a company can generate through the use of a sophisticated marketing and selling application. This ROI model sets a new standard for how companies should evaluate the impact of interactive marketing and self-service applications.

The core premise of the model is that customers who can't find answers to their questions cost companies money. This premise asserts that customers who can't find adequate information on the site:

- **Buy less on-line.** Conversion rates on-line hover around an average of 3.4%. Sites that achieve higher rates can attribute that success to improved navigation, easy access to detailed product information, and answers to customers purchase questions about warranties, shipping costs, and returns.

- **Buy less off-line.** Customers often turn to the Web to research purchases they intend to make off-line. According to Forrester Research, 46% of US households had recently (over a period of three months) researched purchases online but bought them off-line. Furthermore, just over one quarter of retailers say that 25% or more of offline sales are sparked by their Web sites. This means that a site which fails to satisfy customers' needs has an impact on off-line sales.

- **Make contacts through more costly channels.** Not only do live interactions via phone or e-mail cost more than Web self-service, a poorly handled self-service interaction means duplicated costs and lower customer satisfaction. Companies with inadequate self-service pay not only for that cost of interaction, but also for the live contact that follows when customers cannot answer their questions. Forrester Research estimates that a poorly performing self-service effort costs a company $0.38 more than interactions that began on the phone.

This ROI model uses data culled from existing InQuira clients and from industry benchmarks, but allows a company to use its own data. The Interactive Marketing or pre-sales model focuses on expected gains in conversion, both on-line and off-line, from InQuira 6's question-answering accuracy and business rules that allow robust merchandising. The Self-Service or post-sales model focuses largely on cost-savings from the deflection of contacts from more costly assisted-service channels like the phone or e-mail.

Customer Self-Service ROI: Customer Call Deflection

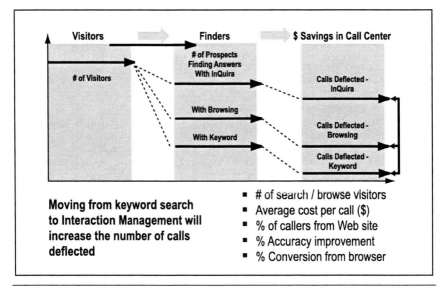

Figure A.1. Moving from keyword search and browse to Customer Search and Navigation helps increase online sales and reduce call center costs.

Pre-Sales ROI

The pre-sales Interactive Marketing portion of InQuira's ROI Model is intended to provide executives with an idea of the impact that InQuira 6 will have on both the revenue and costs of <u>sales and marketing</u> activities in their organizations. InQuira has organized the key pre-sales assumptions we used in this model into a set of core assumptions (Step 1) whose answers drive the output (Steps 2-4). By tailoring the answers to each question to their company, users of the model can produce an ROI estimate unique to their requirements. To estimate the total ROI a company can expect from improving self-service search, we broke down the process into four phases: 1) Data Input, 2) Revenue Impact, 3) Cost Savings, and 4) Overall ROI.

Step 1: Assumptions

InQuira's model allows companies to enter assumptions in four categories: Sales Statistics, the Web's Off-line Influence, Sale's Support Costs, and General Navigation information.

- **Sales Statistics.** Companies will likely have specific information for assumptions regarding sales performance, such as annual sales revenue, percentages of sales through each channel, annual customer value, churn, and average conversion rate.

- **Web's Off-line Influence.** InQuira includes in its model a set of assumptions about the influence of customers' Web experience on their off-line behavior. Studies show not only that customers go to the Web to research products they intend to buy off-line, but that their on-line patrons tend to buy more than their off-line only customers. Thus, the model asks for data about off-line buyers' behavior, such as the percentage who research on-line, the number who are influenced by their on-line experience, and the purchase size over the phone and at stores. For firms that are unsure about certain data, InQuira has provided benchmarks taken from analyst, consulting, and research groups nationwide.

- **Sales Support Costs.** Like the sales statistics above, companies will likely have specific data regarding the volume and cost of e-mails and phone calls which are pre-sales related (as opposed to post-sales support related).

- **General Navigation.** Critical to InQuira's model are assumptions about the success and failure of customers' ability to find information. Based on existing industry research, InQuira assumes that most people browse, and when they fail, they turn to search. Data from User Interface Engineering <www.uie.com> suggest that only 54% find adequate content from browsing through categories and only 34% of customers find information from searching for a combined 70% success rate. Assuming that InQuira raises just the search accuracy rate to 90%, combined browse and search success climbs to 95%.

Step 2: Revenue Impact Results

Step 2 outlines the on-line and off-line revenue impact of improving customers' ability to find adequate information on the site.

Increased conversion rates and market basket size.
Customers largely turn to search when browsing fails. However, on most sites, search also fails. By improving search success for those who use it, companies improve the total percentage of people finding what they need by approximately 20%. Keeping the conversion rate constant on this 20% of new people who now find content, the model predicts that overall conversion will raise from 4% to 5.2%. Furthermore, companies that use the business rules to cross-sell and merchandise products within the results set can expect an extra 20% lift in total purchase size. Thus, our example firm would realize $427,000 annually in extra sales on-line.

Indirect off-line sales impact. Since some customers make purchase decisions based on online research that they will execute off-line, InQuira's model accounts for improvements in this group's ability to answer their questions adequately. Similar calculations are made on conversion rates and market basket size for customers who eventually purchase in the store or over the phone. Because off-line sales remain the purchase channel of choice, our example firm would earn an additional $705,000 annually in extra sales off-line.

Sales Statistics
Total annual sales
Average sale size (market basket)
Online conversion rate
New customer life-time value
Online Impact
Current search accuracy
Accuracy improvement
Prospects using search per month
New conversion rate of online prospects
% Unsatisfied prospects who don't call
Offline Impact
Conversion rate of off-line prospects

Step 3: Cost Savings Results

Step 3 calculates the savings a firm can expect from call center and e-mail deflection by improving the number of people who answer their own questions on-line through self-service. This calculation is made only of pre-sales inquiries, not post-sales support contacts. The model for our example finds that a company would save $43,000 annually using InQuira 6.

Step 4: Overall Pre-Sales ROI

Step 4 in the model combines the calculations in previous steps to show a total pre-sales ROI for InQuira. The model shows that our example firm would realize $1.2 million annually in combined revenue and savings from implementing InQuira 6.

Modeling Post-Sales ROI

InQuira's post-sales (i.e.: self-service) ROI Model focuses on the cost savings companies can expect by deflecting contacts from more expense service channels like e-mail and telephone. InQuira takes a close look at customer behavior, based on experience with existing clients, to determine the number of calls or e-mails deflected as a result of customers finding accurate answers.

Cost per call
Average cost per call
Accuracy improvement
Current search accuracy
Accuracy improvement
Prospects using search per month
% Unsatisfied prospects who don't call
Savings
$ Saved from call deflection per month

Call Deflection Cost Savings

InQuira's model uses as a baseline a Web site that attracts 2.5 million visitors per month, of which only 5% use search. The model assumes that 25% of customers decide to call a support number if they can't find adequate information on the site. With these conservative estimates and an average $6 cost per phone call, a company will save $3.38 million per year by improving the accuracy of search with InQuira 6.

Continuous Improvement for Long-Term ROI

Modeling ROI just begins the first year of implementation. InQuira 6's built-in analytics lets a company analyze customer behavior and incrementally improve their Web site to achieve incrementally higher returns year after year. InQuira's reporting on customer intents and content quality provide companies with insights to improve the ability to answer questions and increase conversion rates.

Three types of reports help companies maximize ROI of their self-service application:

- *Customer Insight Reports.* These reports provide and overview of customers' needs and behavior. Data about hot questions, hot concepts, intents, and product questions give companies the equivalent of a 24x7 focus group.

- *Content Diagnostics Reports.* When no content exists to answer customers' questions, these reports will alert managers that new information is needed. These reports give companies feedback on issues such as problem words, language usage, and document usage.

- *System Metrics Reports.* These reports give managers continuous oversight over the performance of the system. Information about system usage, performance, accuracy, and visitor breakdown alert companies to subtle shifts in customer behavior.

In addition to pre-packaged reports, InQuira 6 provides advanced analytics via OLAP (Online Analytical Processing). InQuira's OLAP capability allows managers to investigate customer behavior across multiple dimensions with alternative "points of view". This means companies investigate behavior trends, rather than simply looking at past transaction data. Furthermore, the powerful analysis capability of InQuira's OLAP engine obviates the need for multiple versions of reports—managers can easily update and change reports as the business needs change.

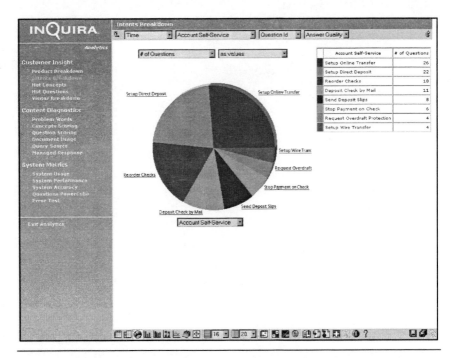

Figure A.2. Powerful analytics built into InQuira 6 give companies visual information about customer behavior instantly. Managers can monitor customer intents, content usage, and system performance to make informed decisions about how best to interact with visitors.

InQuira 6 Product Overview

The InQuira 6 customer search and navigation application is the latest version of the company's flagship software for transforming business Web sites into powerful tools for acquiring new customers, cross-selling and up-selling products and services, reducing the number and cost of service incidents, and driving customer satisfaction.

Using a natural language query interface, InQuira 6 intelligently interprets and then responds to the user's real intent with pinpoint-accurate answers to their specific questions, links to additional information, and opportunities to purchase other related products and services. And, InQuira 6 is enterprise-friendly: fast to install, economical to maintain, and smart enough to report meaningfully on user activities at the site.

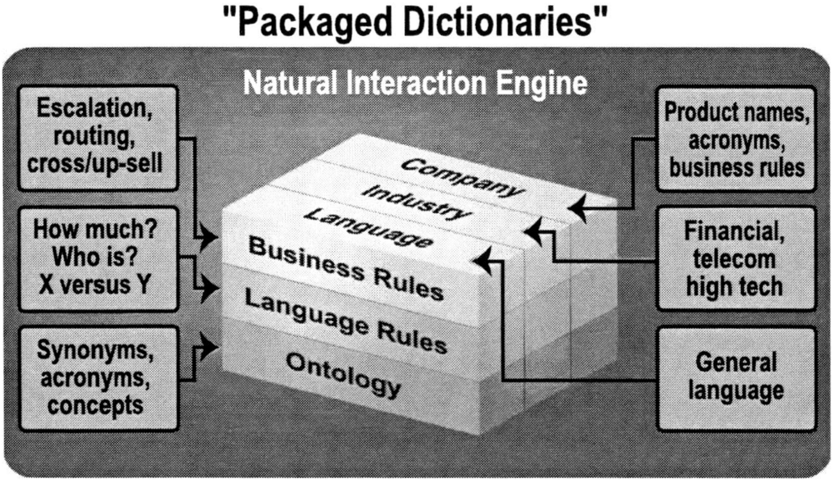

"Packaged Dictionaries"

Figure A.3. InQuira 6's packaged language and industry dictionaries enable low-cost deployment and give users a better online experience than keyword search.

InQuira 6 is setting a new standard for customer-facing Web search solutions with the introduction of its standard-setting Dynamic Navigation User Interface (UI), a unique search return Web page that helps the site visitor quickly understand and easily explore all the content the site has to offer that's relevant to their original question. And, InQuira 6 goes far beyond simply returning search results; advanced business rules and analytics give businesses control over customer dialogs and the ability to present cross-sell and up-sell opportunities, resulting in 'high touch' service and increased revenues—all at a low cost.

Contact Us:

InQuira Inc.
851 Traeger Avenue, Suite 125
San Bruno, CA 94066
T: 650-246-5000
F: 650-246-5036

For sales inquiries: <sales@InQuira.com>
For product support: <support@InQuira.com>

artificial intelligence: tools and algorithms for automated learning and reasoning.

case-based reasoning (CBR): a technology that has existed for two decades. It attempts to mimic the problem-solving ability of a human through artificial intelligence. This technology utilizes a static series of questions and answers to arrive at a predefined solution.

clickstream analysis: analysis of the path a customer takes through a particular Web site.

closed-loop knowledge exchange: organizations that offer Web self-service can gather electronic customer feedback on new products, concepts, and/or the customer's service experience. The idea is to get quick feedback, learn from that, and then act on it to improve.

co-browsing: technology that allows a CSR to see the same screen that the customer does as the customer is viewing it.

contact center: more than a call center. This organization of people responds to customer needs through multi-media channels such as e-mail, Web self-service, assisted-service, chat, etc.

CRM (customer relationship management): the process of ensuring that an organization creates loyal, rather than just satisfied, customers. Includes a wide variety of strategies, systems, and initiatives.

customer escalation: the process where a customer's issue is forwarded up to the appropriate service channel for resolution. The focus is on a seamless customer experience while using only the appropriate level of resources required by the customer to get resolution to their issue.

customer profiling: finding groups of like-minded customers and segmenting them into common groups.

data warehouses: collections of logically organized data sources suitable for organizational-level business decisions support.

decision tree (a.k.a. diagnostic tree): a static series of questions and corresponding answers that guide the user to a predefined solution to his/her query.

dynamic content generation: the automated ability of a knowledge base to grow as customers ask and get answers to questions never addressed before.

e-mail alias: this is a designated e-mail address where customers can send their e-mail.

explicit knowledge: knowledge that is fully and clearly expressed and leaves nothing implied. FAQs are one type of explicit knowledge.

FAQ (frequently asked questions): a body of knowledge that can increase organizational efficiency by documenting and utilizing the most commonly asked customer questions. This information is typically paired with a search engine and allows customers to search for their own answers rather than rely on CSRs.

hosted solution: hiring a vendor to manage your Web site.

IVR (interactive voice response): a computerized phone system that reacts to the digits customers key or to their voice. Similar to the way a computer reacts to the click of a mouse or keystrokes.

IWR (interactive Web response): a computerized electronic system that reacts to customers' key strokes and/or click of their mouse.

keyword matching: this search mechanism requires customers to type in words or a series of words in a search box. The result will be the return of a large number of relevant and irrelevant links. This mechanism can't discern the customer's intent but searches for words that are actually in a Web page.

knowledge base (a.k.a. Web-based knowledge optimization platform): repositories of content that typically include a search engine that lets customers locate information that relates to their request for service.

licensed solution: the purchase of software that allows the organization to support its own Web site.

multi-channel customer service: channels can include: chat, e-mail, Web self-service and assisted-service, live CSR support, and/or kiosk offerings.

natural language processing (NLP): is powered by dictionary-based search engines. These search engines analyze questions, discern the important words and sentence structure, and match them to the text of stored documents. This technology utilizes linguistic techniques to discern subtle relationships among concepts. They have the ability to interpret the customer's question as well as the text on stored documents.

natural language query engine (a.k.a. natural language interface): this allows customers to enter their questions in natural terms, such as "What are your hours of operation?" rather than by key words such as "store hours?" A list of Frequently Asked Questions (as well as the coordinated answers) as well as other company databases support the information retrieval system that is done by keyword or pattern matching of the questions' most important words.

proof point: vendors' proof that they can deliver the results they promise.

ROI (return on investment): an organization's ability to recoup the cost of an investment.

routing rule: much like a call center's business logic, this is part of an e-mail management system.

tacit knowledge: knowledge that is understood without being openly stated. Corporate best practices and skills obtained on the job are two examples of tacit knowledge.

text retrieval systems: these offer a basic database of technical reference documents that can be installed and maintained at affordable costs. A CSR can search the data base, typically using a keyword search, for the answer to a customer's query. Finding the pertinent information becomes more time consuming and difficult as the data base grows.

ticket box: much like a queue in a call center, this is part of an e-mail management system.

user: much like a CSR in a call center, this is part of an e-mail management system.

vertical market: a specific industry, such as the financial services industry or hospitality industry.

virtual agent: a computer-generated CSR designed to assist customers with their service needs.

voIP: voice over Internet Protocol; allows customers to use their voice, rather than the pushing of buttons, to move through the steps of their service interaction.

Web collaboration: a technology set that includes chat, online meetings, co-browsing, remote diagnostics, and repair. These technologies when used with Web self-service offer customers real-time service and support.

"A Blueprint for Strategic eBusiness/Call Center Integration: A 10-Step Guide." *Kramer and Associates Newsletter*.

Analyst View. <www.imakenews.com/primus1/e article000078452.cfm. 2002>.

Anton, Jon, Brian James, and Jim Small. "The Best Service is Often Self-Service." *Customer Relationship Management* no. 2: (1996).

Apicella, Mario and David L. Margulius. "CRM Daily Dot Com: At Your Own Service." (2003).

Bocklund, Lori. "The Customer Contact Center: Changing Times, Changing Paradigms. How Will You Respond?" *Vanguard Communications* (1999).

Caisse, Kimberly B. "Forget Self-Service – Hone the Phone." *CRMDaily Dot Com* (2002).

Caisse, Kimberly B.: "Online Chat – No Breakthrough for Customer Service." *CRMDaily Dot Com* (2002).

Caisse, Kimberly.: "Holding These Truths to Be CRM Self-Service." *CRM Daily Dot Com* (2002).

Dawson, Keith.: "The Web and Call Centers." *Call Center News Service* (2000).

Dietz, C. Alex.: "Making CRM Work Through Customer Data Integration." Acxiom Products (2001).

Microsoft. "Enabling the Government Knowledge Worker." *Microsoft Insight* (2002). <www.mircosoft.com/europe/insight/government/keynotes/item124.html>.

eGain, *Winning in the Global Marketplace,* 2001.

"e service." eGain Communications White Paper. <www.egain.com>.

Gianforte, Greg.: "The Insider's Guide to Next-Generation Customer Service on the Web." *RightNow Technologies* (2002).

Gianforte, Greg.: "The Insider's Guide to Customer Service on the Web." White paper, RightNow Technologies (2001).

Hiatt, Jeff.: "World-class Call Centers – the Next Generation." Call Center Learning Center (2002).

Hill, Kimberly. "Meeting the Multichannel Service Challenge." *CRM Daily Dot Com* (2002).

Hirsh, Lou. "All Customers Are Not Created Equal." *CRM Daily Dot Com* (2002).

Hirsh, Lou. "Is Online Self-Service Really Service?" *CRMDaily Dot Com* (2002).

Hollowell, Todd. "Focus on the Customer." *Insurancetech.com* (2002).

Homan, David. "Look Past Products to Web Services' True Promise." *Information Week* (2002).

Honeycomb, Jeff. "Insider's Guide to the Key Elements of a Complete Internet Customer Service Solution." White paper. RightNow Technologies (2001).

"Secrets to Wooing Your Online Customers." Inc.com <www.inc.com> (1999).

"Interactions: The Foundation of Business Relationships." White paper. eGain Communications <www.egain.com>.

iPhrase <www.iphrase.com/solutions/employee.html>.

Jupiter Consumer Survey Report: "The State of Customer Service, 2003." *Customer Relationship Management* (March 2003).

Jupiter CRM Model, 12/02 (US only). © 2003 Jupiter Research, a division of Jupitermedia Corporation.

Jupiter Research (4/03). © 2003 Jupiter Research, a division of Jupitermedia Corporation.

Jupiter Self-service Model, 4/02 (US only). © 2003 Jupiter Research, a division of Jupitermedia Corporation.

Jupiter Market Forecast Report: "CRM Through 2008." *Customer Relationship Management* (February 21, 2003).

Kaneshige, Tom. "Greasing the Contact Center Machine." *CRMDaily Dot Com* (2002).

Kasravi, Kas. "Advances in Knowledge Management: An Information Technology Viewpoint".

Kyle, Dennis. "Call Center Technology Solutions: Deploying IVR/IWR to Meet Customer Self-Service Needs." (1999).

Lieber, Mitchell. "Target Marketing: Can We Chat – About Web Chat?" (2002).

Margulius, David L. "Workflow meets BPM." *Infoworld.com* (2002).

<www.microsoft.com/europe/insight/Government/Keynotes/item24.html>

Morphy, Erika. "Weaning Customers from Live Support." *CRMDaily Dot Com* (2002).

Nunley, Roger H. "Customer Service Doesn't Cut It Anymore." (2002).

Perez, Jeanette. "Intelligent Enterprise: Help Yourself." (2002).

Philonenko, Laurent. "The Future of the Customer-Focused Enterprise." TMC net.com (2002).

"Providing a Superior User Experience with Web Self-Service." Primus Knowledge Solutions. White paper, (2001).

Rabin, Steve. "Profiling Customers and Creating Meaningful Segments for eCommerce." *CommerceNet* (October 1999).

Raizada, Sanjay. "Eleven Steps to Success in Data Warehousing." Syntel

"Real-Time Service and Support." White paper. eGain Communications <www.egain.com>.

"Remedy Integration." White paper. eGain Communications <www.egain.com> (2001).

Robinson, Teri. "Slashing the Costs of Self-Service Programs." *CRM Daily Dot Com* (2002).

Rosenberg, Art. "The Future of Contact Center Self-Service." CommWeb.com (2002).

Rufo, Joanie. "If You Build it, Will They Come? Getting the Most Out of Self-Service Systems." *AMR Research* (2003).

Srikanth, Anjana. "Performing Workplace: Longest Broadway Run." (2002).

Steul, Don and Steve Bell. "The New Blended Contact Center: Call Blending and Media Integration in the Internet-Enabled Contact Center." TMCnet.com (2003).

"The Insider's Guide to e-service Best Practices: 15 Best Practices Smart Companies Use to Maximize the Business Benefits of Customer Service on the Web." RightNow Technologies, (2002).

Thompson, Bob. "Strategies for Success in the Customer Age." RightNow Technologies (2002).

Tobin, Tom. "The Value of Online Self-Service." White paper ServiceWare (2002).

"UK Companies Adopt Web Self-Service in Droves, But Fail Miserably in Quality of Answers." eGain Communications (2001).

Van Everen, David. "Customer Segmentation Strategies." Line56 (2002).

Verma, Gaurav and Todd Hollowell. "CRM Makes Strides in Self-Service." *Information Week* (2002).

Warner, Doug. "The Insider's Guide to Building an Effective Knowledgebase." RightNow Technologies (2000).

Watson, James K. Jr. "The Economies of Web Self-Service Finding a Low-cost Method of Customer Service." *Ecomworld* (2002).

"Web Self-Service." Information Service.com. <www.informationselfservice.com/general_presentations.asp>.

"What is Knowledge Management?" Sun Microsoftsystems, Inc.

"Workplace Performance Tools." *Business Rules*, Revision 1.3 (2001).

"Your Self-Service Solution: Buy or Build?" Netkey, Inc. (2002).

Co-Author

Dr. Jon Anton (also known as "Dr. Jon") is the director of benchmark research at Purdue University's Center for Customer-Driven Quality. He specializes in enhancing customer service strategy through inbound call centers, and e-business centers, using the latest in telecommunications (voice), and computer (digital) technology. He also focuses on using the Internet for external customer access, as well as Intranets and middleware.

Since 1995, Dr. Jon has been the principal investigator of the Purdue University Call Center Benchmark Research. This data is now collected at the BenchmarkPortal.com Web site, where it is placed into a data warehouse that currently contains over ten million data points on call center performance. Based on the analysis of this data, Dr. Jon authors the following monthly publications: "The Purdue Page" in *Call Center Magazine*, "Dr. Jon's Benchmarks" in *Call Center News*, "Dr. Jon's Industry Statistics" in *Customer Interface Magazine*, and "Dr. Jon's Business Intelligence" in the *Call Center Manager's Report*.

Dr. Jon has assisted over 400 companies in improving their customer service strategy/delivery by the design and implementation of inbound and outbound call centers, as well as in the decision-making process of using teleservice providers for maximizing service levels while minimizing costs per call. In August of 1996, *Call Center Magazine* honored Dr. Jon by selecting him as an Original Pioneer of the emerging call center industry. In October of 2000, Dr. Jon was named to the Call Center Hall of Fame. In January of 2001, Dr. Jon was selected for the industry's "Leaders and Legends" Award by Help Desk 2000. Dr. Jon is also a member of the National Committee for Quality Assurance.

Dr. Jon has guided corporate executives in strategically re-positioning their call centers as robust customer access centers through a combination of benchmarking, re-engineering, consolidation, outsourcing, and Web-enablement. The resulting single point of contact for the customer allows business to be conducted anywhere, anytime, and in any form. By better understanding the customer lifetime value, Dr. Jon has developed techniques for calculating the ROI for customer service initiatives.

Dr. Jon has published 96 papers on customer service and call center methods in industry journals. In 1997, one of his papers on self-service was awarded the best article of the year by *Customer Relationship Management Magazine*.

Dr. Jon has published twenty-three professional books:

Enabling IVR Self-Service with Speech Recognition, The Anton Press, 2003

Managing Web-Based Customer Experiences: Self-Service Integrated with Assisted Service, The Anton Press, 2003

From Cost to Profit Center: How Technology Enables the Difference, The Anton Press, 2003

Customer Service and the Human Experience: We, the People, Make a Difference, The Anton Press, 2003

Customer Service at a Crossroads: What You Do Next to Improve Performance Will Determine Your Company's Destiny, The Anton Press, 2003

Offshore Outsourcing Opportunities, The Anton Press, 2002

Optimizing Outbound Calling: The Strategic Use of Predictive Dialers, The Anton Press, 2002

Customer Relationship Management Technology: Building the Infrastructure for Customer Collaboration, The Anton Press, 2002

Customer Obsession: Your Roadmap to Profitable CRM, The Anton Press, 2002

Integrating People with Process and Technology, The Anton Press, 2002

Selecting a Teleservices Partner, The Anton Press, 2002

How to Conduct a Call Center Performance Audit: A to Z, The Anton Press, 2002

20:20 CRM A Visionary Insight into Unique Customer Contact, The Anton Press, 2001

Minimizing Agent Turnover, The Anton Press, 2001

e-Business Customer Service, The Anton Press, 2001

Customer Relationship Management, The Bottom Line to Optimizing Your ROI, Prentice Hall, 2nd Edition, 2001

Call Center Performance Enhancement Using Simulation and Modeling, Purdue University Press, 2000

Call Center Benchmarking: How Good is "Good Enough", Purdue University Press, 1999

Listening to the Voice of the Customer, Alexander Communications, 1997

Contact Center Management by the Numbers, Purdue University Press, 1997

Customer Relationship Management: Making Hard Decisions with Soft Numbers, Prentice-Hall, Inc., 1996

Inbound Customer Contact Center Design, Dame Publishers, Inc., 1994

Computer-Assisted Learning, Hafner Publishing, Inc., 1985

Dr. Jon is the editor for a series of professional books entitled *Customer Access Management*, published by the Purdue University Press.

Dr. Jon's formal education was in technology, including a Doctorate of Science and a Master of Science from Harvard University, a Master of Science from the University of Connecticut, and a Bachelor of Science from the University of Notre Dame. He also completed a three-summer intensive Executive Education program in Business at the Graduate School of Business at Stanford University.

Dr. Jon can be reached at 765.494.8357 or at <DrJonAnton@BenchmarkPortal.com>.

Co-Author

Michael Murphy is the President and Chief Executive Officer of InQuira. Mike brings over 20 years of technology management and sales experience to his role as CEO of InQuira, Inc. Mike started InQuira in 2002 with a goal of developing a solution that would set new standards of functionality and commercial viability for Web-based customer search and navigation. Mike is now spearheading InQuira's aggressive move to deliver online interactive marketing and customer self-service applications to industry leaders like Bank of America, BEA and AT&T. Prior to InQuira, Mike served as one of four key executives at Cambridge Technology Partners (CTP), where he grew the Western Region from revenues of $8M in 1995 to $80M in 1998. Mike then oversaw CTP's sales, marketing, alliances and partner programs, totaling more than $400M in revenue. Prior to his tenure at CTP, Mike spent 13 years at Hewlett Packard. He holds a BA in Management from Loyola Marymount University.

Content Editor

 **Anita Rockwell** is the Director of Business Intelligence at BenchmarkPortal, Inc. She is a Purdue University certified contact center auditor specializing in assisting contact center managers in optimally integrating people with processes and technology. Anita's primary passion is around creating the optimal environment in the contact center, with a special emphasis on the dynamics required to release the potential of each team member. In 2001, Anita co-authored a popular professional book called, "Minimizing Agent Turnover" with Dr. Jon Anton.

Anita's other core competencies include all of the following human resource challenges: 1) recruiting and screening, 2) hiring and training, 3) employee development, 4) organizational structure, 5) agent monitoring, coaching, and motivation, 6) change management, customer satisfaction surveys, and finally 7) agent quality measurement and benchmarking.

Anita has also developed a proven methodology to first discover the root causes of workflow process problems in a customer service contact center (including telephone and e-mails), and then to recommend specific solutions to improve efficiency and effectiveness to acceptable, best practice levels.

Anita was the Vice President of Customer Service with Simon Delivers.com where she designed, implemented, and managed an inbound customer service contact center for customer support.

Anita also spent sixteen years with the Blue Cross and Blue Shield of Minnesota where she was quickly promoted to Vice President of Customer Service, which included all aspects of customer contact management. In this capacity she was responsible for over 1 million members, 235 employees, 7 regional offices and an annual budget of over $10 million. Anita lists the following as her major accomplishments while with the Blue Cross and Blue Shield organization:

1. Re-organized the division, and championed technology enhancements.

2. Increased percent of inquiries resolved on first contact by 20%.

3. Increased customer satisfaction for regional service team from 75% to 87% in less than a year.

4. Dramatically reduced service employee turnover rate from over 50% to under 10% and improved employee satisfaction to a level 15% above the company average.

5. Developed and piloted first Intelligent Customer Service Workstation to streamline service delivery.

6. Increased market share in the region she managed grew from 45.5% to 49.5%.

7. Developed innovative client review tool that resulted in the identification of 250 initiatives to improve service.

8. Developed, implemented and directed one of the company's first successful pay-for-performance initiatives which increased claims productivity by over 20% while incurring no additional costs.

9. Developed processes and tools that enhanced effectiveness of the team resulting in the retention of key provider partners and turning around the satisfaction ratings of the providers with her company.

10. Worked directly with a Senior Vice President and CIO and other senior staff members on key corporate projects as part of the company's overall performance improvement strategy.

Anita graduated Cum Laude from Bethel College with a Bachelors Degree in Business Management with an emphasis in Organizational Studies. She is also currently working toward her Masters in psychology.

Anita can be reached at 651.755-1210 or at <AnitaRockwell@BenchmarkPortal.com>.

Technical Writer/Editor

Cory Gideon Gunderson is a free-lance technical writer and editor. During her call center years, she partnered with leadership to improve customer satisfaction through soft skill training, coaching, and communication initiatives.

Cory writes and edits technical books and has written company newsletters, magazine articles, and political campaign literature and speeches. She has also written Juvenile Nonfiction books that were published for the library and school markets.

Cory has worked in the Aviation, Financial Services, and Health Care industries. In addition to writing and editing, her areas of passion and expertise include Human Resources, Training, and Customer Service. Cory can be reached at <gundys4@cs.com>.

A

American Customer
  Satisfaction Index, 6
automated pharmacy, 36
automated teller machine
  (ATM), 33, 41

B

Bank of America, 111, 123,
  125
BellSouth, 123, 124
Borders Books, 16
Broad Daylight, 124
business objectives, 9, 66, 69,
  71, 79, 80

C

Call Center Learning Center
  study, 28
case-based reasoning, 57, 58,
  141
chat, 9, 61, 72, 73, 75, 85, 88,
  104, 141, 142, 144
Chatham, Bob, ix
co-browse, 62
Continuous Improvement, 80
CRM Guru study, 7
customer satisfaction, 2, 3, 4,
  6, 13, 19, 30, 36, 63, 83, 86,
  93
segmentation, 92, 94

D

Daniels, David, xi, 107
data warehousing, 102
Delphi Group study, 88
Doculabs, 30

E

e-mail, 7, 9, 10, 12, 13, 14, 15,
  19, 29, 54, 57, 61, 63, 65, 72,
  75, 82, 84, 85, 88, 90, 93,
  104, 141, 142, 143
escalation, 73, 141
explicit sources of information,
  100
External Facing Knowledge
  Base, 95

F

FAQ, 83, 84, 95, 98, 100, 142
first time resolution, 40
Forrester Research, 59
Forrester Research study, 13,
  29

G

Gartner Group, 14
gas pump, 35
Giga Research, 58

H

Harvard Business Review
  study, 4
Hewson Consulting, 95
Hiatt, Jeff, 28

I

implementation, 2, 20, 59, 66,
  67, 71, 74, 75, 80
integration, 6, 57, 58, 63, 66,
  72, 88, 90
Internal Facing Knowledge
  Base, 101
Intuit Corporation, 48

20:20 CRM A Visionary insight into unique customer contacts
The contact center is at the heart of many businesses today, and CRM initiatives are making customer contact even more critical to the health of every company. 20:20 CRM provides a strategic view of where businesses should be going with their customer contact operation, with practical examples of how to get there.
ISBN 0-9630464-5-4　　　　　　　*By: Dr. Jon Anton and Laurent Philonenko*　**Price: $24.95**

Benchmarking for Profits! BenchmarkPortal's Guide to Improve Your Contact Center, Your Career and Your Company
Done right, and done regularly, benchmarking provides improved work life, career advancement and substantially increased earnings on a consistent basis. This book is an essential manual for continuous improvement peer group benchmarking that shows convincingly why proper professionalism in today's environment requires benchmarking. Includes valuable information on how to benchmark through BenchmarkPortal and describes the latest products to help you get the most from this crucial activity.
ISBN 0-9719652-1-8　　　　　　　By: Bruce Belfiore with Dr. Jon Anton　**Price: $11.95**

Call Center Benchmarking "How 'good' is good enough?"
This "how to" book describes the essential steps of benchmarking a call center with other similar call centers, with an emphasis on "self assessment." The reader learns how to plan a benchmark, how to collect the correct performance data, how to analyze the data, and how to find improvement initiatives based on the findings.
ISBN 1-55753-215-X　　　　　　　　　　　　*By: Dr. Jon Anton*　**Price: $39.95**

Call Center Performance Enhancement - Using Simulation and Modeling
This book provides its readers with an understanding about the role, value, and practical deployment of simulation - an exciting technology for the planning, management, and analysis of call centers. The book provides useful guidelines to call center analysts, managers, and consultants who may be investigating or are considering the use of simulation as a vehicle in their business to responsibly manage change.
ISBN 1-55753-182-X　　　　　　　*By: Jon Anton, Vivek Bapat, Bill Hall*　**Price: $48.95**

Customer Obsession: Your Roadmap to Profitable CRM
Finally, here is a book that covers the complete "journey" of CRM implementation. Ad Nederlof and Dr. Jon Anton have done the near impossible: to position CRM in such a way that it makes practical sense to C-level executives. Beginning with the title of the book, "Customer Obsession," on through the last chapter, this book positions CRM for what it really is, namely, a complete change in corporate strategy, from the top down, that brings the customer into focus.
ISBN 0-9719652-0-X　　　　　　　*By: Ad Nederlof and Dr. Jon Anton*　**Price: $24.95**

Customer Relationship Management: The Bottom Line to Optimizing Your ROI
Customer Relationship Management recommends effective initiatives toward improving customer service and managing change. Creative methodologies are geared toward building relationships through customer-perceived value instruments, monitoring customer relationship indices, and changing the corporate culture and the way people work.
ISBN 0-13-099069-8　　　　　　*By Dr. Jon Anton and Natalie L. Petouhoff*　**Price: $33.33**

Also Available from The Anton Press

Customer Relationship Management Technology: Building the Infrastructure for Customer Collaboration

From our research on the American consumer, it has become very clear that potentially the best customer service strategy is "to offer every possible channel for the customer to help themselves, i.e., self-service." Customer actuated service is mostly driven by technology, and the "art" of self-service is to ensure that the technology is intuitive, easy to use, and that the customer is rewarded for "having done the job themselves." This book delves into all the technology solutions that enable self-service. The reader will find a robust description of the technology alternatives, and many examples of how self-service is saving companies money, while at the same time satisfying customers.

ISBN 0-9630464-7-0 *By Dr. Jon Anton and Bob Vilsoet* **Price: $39.99**

Customer Service and the Human Experience: We, the People, Make the Difference

One of the leading challenges for today's managers is the training and motivating of excellent agents. While much attention has been focused on the technology and benefits of providing multiple channels for customer contact, little attention has been paid to handling the human part of the equation—training CSRs to field more than just telephone communications. Great statistics and benchmarking help the customer service/call center professional keep ahead of the ever-changing business environment as the authors successfully blend the critical human aspect of the center with the ever growing need for metrics and the bottom line.

ISBN 0-9719652-7-7 *By Dr. Rosanne D'Ausilio and Dr. Jon Anton* **Price: $34.95**

Customer Service at a Crossroads: What You Do Next to Improve Performance Will Determine Your Company's Destiny

By consistently delivering information about products, services and information to customer service agents, based on their individual skill levels—at the right time in the right way, organizations are also delivering a consistent, clear understanding of corporate objectives and vision. The result: thousands of customer interactions that delight the customer and improve retention as well as corporate profitability. Optimizing agent performance can quickly deliver incredible returns beyond customer loyalty. That is what this book is all about.

ISBN 0-9719652-6-9 *By Matt McConnell and Dr. Jon Anton* **Price: $15.95**

e-Business Customer Service: The Need for Quality Assessment

With the advent of e-business technology, we suddenly find ourselves with completely different customer service channels. The old paradigms are gone forever. This books details how to measure and manage e-business customer service. The book describes the key performance indicators for these new channels, and it describes how to manage by these new rules of engagement with specific metrics. Managing customer service in this "new age" is different, it is challenging, and it is impossible to migrate from the old to the new without reading this book.

ISBN 0-9630464-9-7 *By Dr. Jon Anton and Michael Hoeck* **Price: $44.00**

From Cost to Profit Center: How Technology Enables the Difference

This book is a series of case studies in which we collected performance metrics before and after implementation of specific technology solutions for call centers. In each case study we saw varying levels of improvement, and were then able to quantify the financial impact in terms of ROS, and in some cases, in terms of earnings per share. For call center managers contemplating the addition of new call center technology, this book will be an asset in better understanding the impact of technology in enabling higher performance.

ISBN 0-9719652-8-5 *By Dr. Jon Anton and R. Scott Davis* **Price: $44.95**

How to Conduct a Call Center Performance Audit: A to Z

Call centers are an important company asset, but also a very expensive one. By learning to conduct a performance audit, readers will be able to understand over fifty specific aspects of a call center that must be running smoothly in order to achieve maximum performance in both efficiency and effectiveness of handling inbound customer calls.

ISBN 0-9630464-6-2   *By Dr. Jon Anton and Dru Phelps* **Price: $34.99**

Integrating People with Process and Technology: Gaining Employee Acceptance of Technology Initiatives

This book contains valuable information regarding the "people" side of technology initiatives. Many companies buy the best hardware and software, and spend thousands of dollars implementing technology only to find out that the employees resist the changes, and do not fully adopt the new, and possibly, improved processes. By understanding how to manage people during change, managers will see a much quicker ROI on their technology initiatives.

ISBN 0-9630464-3-8   *By Jon Anton, Natalie Petouhoff, & Lisa Schwartz* **Price: $39.99**

Listening to the Voice of the Customer

With the help of this book, the professional skills you need to measure customer satisfaction will lead you to different approaches until you have found the one that best fits you, your company, and your organization's culture.

ISBN 0-915910-43-8   *By Dr. Jon Anton* **Price: $33.95**

Managing Web-Based Customer Experiences: Self-Service Integrated with Assisted-Service

The time to grow your call center into a multi-channel customer contact center is now. This book has the power to help you increase customer satisfaction through the implementation of Web self-service. The value of this book can be calculated in terms of calls deflected from your call center, increased customer retention, an ultimately in a healthy return on your investment. In this book, the authors take you step-by-step through the best practices that lead to a successful self and assisted-service strategy.

ISBN 0-9719652-4-2   *By Dr. Jon Anton and Mike Murphy* **Price: $35.95**

Minimizing Agent Turnover: The Biggest Challenge for Customer Contact Centers

Some agent turnover can be functional, but most turnover is dysfunctional and can be very expensive. This book explores the types of turnover, including internal versus external; and documents the typical causes of agent turnover. Most importantly, this book describes a methodology for diagnosing the root causes of your agent turnover, and suggests improvement initiatives to minimize agent turnover at your customer contact center.

ISBN 0-9630464-2-X   *By Dr. Jon Anton and Anita Rockwell* **Price: $39.99**

Offshore Outsourcing Opportunities

For call center executives wanting to explore and understand the benefits of offshore outsourcing, the authors have brought together 'under one cover' a comprehensive guide that takes the reader through each step of the complex issues of outsourcing customer service telephone calls to agents in another country. With the pressure of today's competitive climate forcing companies to take a hard look at providing higher quality customer services at lower costs, this book is a "must read" for every call center executive.

ISBN 0-9719652-3-4   *By Dr. Jon Anton and John Chatterley* **Price: $34.99**

Optimizing Outbound Calling: The Strategic Use of Predictive Dialers

The content of the book is organized in such a way as to assist the reader in understanding the complete end-to-end process of automated outbound call dialing. Specifically, the reader will find the following steps described in detail: a) preparing a needs assessment, b) selecting and contracting a predictive dialer supplier, c) implementing a predictive dialer solution, d) applying change management principles to ensure "buy-in" by existing agents, d) handling and using dialer reports, and finally, e) benchmarking dialer improvements to ensure attaining the anticipated ROI.

ISBN 0-9719652-2-6   *By Jon Anton and Alex G. Demczak*   **Price: $39.99**

Selecting a Teleservices Partner: Sales, Service, and Support

This book tackles one of today's hottest topics: Customer Contact Outsourcing. Companies are in a quandary about the myriad of teleservices questions they're faced with, such as deciding to outsource, cost / benefit analysis, RFP development, proposal assessment, vendor selection, contractual requirements, service level performance measurement, and managing an ongoing teleservices relationship. With the authors help, readers will find this complex issue straightforward to approach, understand, and implement.

ISBN 0-9630464-8-9   *By Jon Anton and Lori Carr*   **Price: $34.99**

The Four-Minute Customer: Getting Jazzed about Your People and Quality Management in Your Call Center

This is a very unique book directed at developing and maintaining "Top Reps" that are uniquely motivated to deliver the highest possible quality of caller customer service at your center. Learn what it takes to find and lead the best of the best. Don't settle for mediocrity. Instead, learn how to manage the best in class customer contact center by attracting and keeping Top Reps at your organization.

ISBN 0-9630464-1-1   *By Michael Tamer*   **Price: $34.99**

Wake Up Your Call Center: Humanizing Your Interaction Hub, 3rd edition

With new and up-to-date material, this third edition speaks volumes about the need to reinforce the human element in the equation. This is a straight forward guide for humanizing the impersonal, with practical to-do's, real life examples, and applications to delight your customers. In depth chapters include mixed messages, change and stress management, conflict resolution, rapport building, and communicating powerfully, just to mention a few.

ISBN 1-55753-217-6   *By Rosanne D'Ausilio, Ph.D*   **Price: $44.95**

Order Form

Secure online ordering is available at: www.benchmarkportal.com/bookstore

Billing Information: **Shipping Information** (if different):

Name	
Company	
Address	
Address 2	
City/St/Zip	
Phone	

Please charge my: _____ **American Express**   _____ **Discover**

           _____ **Mastercard**   _____ **Visa**

Card Number

Expiration Date

Signature

I've enclosed a check in the amount of

Purchase Order Number

Book Title	Amt*	Qty	Total
Books Total			
Shipping and Handling *For all U.S. addresses, $5.00 for the first book, $3.00 for each additional book.* *For all International addresses, books must be **pre-paid** and must include a shipping and handling charge of $25.00 for the first book and $10 for each additional book.*			
Total Amount Due**			

Call for volume and pre-order discounts available (805-614-0123 Ext. 10)
**State sales tax will be added where applicable*

For other books, tapes, and videos visit our online store:

http://www.benchmarkportal.com/bookstore

Send all orders to:
     BenchmarkPortal, Inc.
     3130 Skyway Drive, Suite 702
     Santa Maria, CA 93455-1817
For quick service, fax your order to: (805) 614-0055
For questions about your order, please call: (805) 614-0123 Ext. 10

INDUSTRY REPORTS

Industry Reports Available From BenchmarkPortal, Inc.

Secure online ordering is available at:
http://www.benchmarkportal.com/bookstore

or call (805) 614-0123 Ext. 20

These industry reports contain hundreds of call center benchmarks and best practices for a specific industry:

Aerospace

Airline

All Industries

Automotive

Banking

Brokerage

Cable Television

Catalog

Computer Hardware

Computer Products

Computer Software

Credit Card

Financial Services

Government & Non-Profit

Healthcare Provider

Help Desk

Insurance

Insurance – Health

Insurance – Life

Insurance – Property & Casualty

Outbound Teleservices

Publishing & Media

Retail

Technical Support

Telecommunications

Transportation

Travel & Hospitality

Utilities

Wireless

SERVICES AND PRODUCT LISTING

Services and Product Listing from BenchmarkPortal, Inc.

We provide several options to allow executives to choose the level of service that will optimize their return from the benchmarking exercise.

1. Self-Service Basic Benchmarking

Sign up at our Web site and talk to one of our customer service representatives. Your data can be entered securely online. Detailed, confidential reports showing your competitive performance are e-mailed to you within days of data completion and validation.

Recommended for: All call centers. Centers that do not have sufficient analytical staff are encouraged, but not required, to use a Purdue-certified consultant (see Web site) to help them with data gathering and report interpretation. Centers with their own analytical staff should consider sending us their specialist to receive training in the proper use of our benchmarking reports.

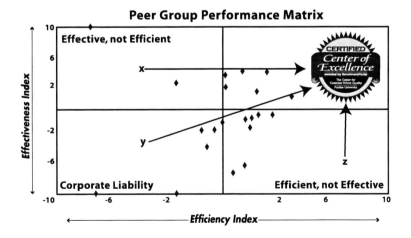

2. Competitive Benchmark Studies

Managers may want to a) see additional metrics that are specific to their sector; and b) know that the peer group is composed of their direct competitors. BenchmarkPortal is the trusted research organization that collects the additional data from all parties and produces the sector-specific report. ONLY anonymous and aggregate data are included as peer information in the reports.

Recommended for: Operations that are part of an identifiable competitive peer sector and that have key performance metrics that are specific to that sector.

> **"With Echo, we now incorporate the 'voice of the customer' into everything we do. We love it."**
> — Joyce Whalen, eBay Director of Customer Experience

BenchmarkPortal introduces a groundbreaking new approach for translating direct customer feedback into rich business intelligence. *Echo ™* incorporates the best practices from 'world-class' companies based on our own extensive benchmarking studies.

Echo ™ challenges the traditional approach to measuring and improving service. The status quo has consistently fallen short of delivering results. Based on our research, we have taken the best practices of the best companies and incorporated them into a dynamic closed-loop approach that really delivers.

Echo ™ provides an all-in-one solution:
- Scientifically-based customer feedback collection
- Primary source for monitoring agent effectiveness
- Service recovery, including post-recovery effectiveness
- Core cause determination and analysis
- Effective, behavior-based agent coaching
- Meaningful metrics to track results
- Real-time Reporting
- Business intelligence needed to make informed decisions

We can help you develop and implement our revolutionary monitoring and coaching approach without loss of precious time in confronting technology and implementation issues. In most cases, we can launch *Echo ™* in just 60 days.

4. Fair-Compare™ Agent Satisfaction Benchmarking

 Finally, BenchmarkPortal introduces a new benchmarking option designed specifically for Contact Centers ...a method to compare the satisfaction results of your Contact Center agents to other Contact Center agents!

As a Contact Center Professional, you know the importance of retaining your talent. Our **Fair-Compare**™ benchmarking surveys and reporting system quickly pinpoint areas of risk to proactively resolve them.

Fair-Compare™ lets you compare your Contact Center agents based on any category captured, including:

- Tenure
- Age-range
- Job Title
- Skill-set
- Supervisor
- And lots more!

Fair-Compare™ provides the ability to compare your Contact Center results to:

- Your Peer Group
- Your Industry
- Best-in-Industry
- Your Demographic Region
- Similar Environments

Customizable, always available, Online Reporting is a central feature of **Fair-Compare**™, providing results that you can act on quickly. Survey results help you pinpoint exact areas to focus on for immediate improvement initiatives, giving you the "Why" behind each "What".

Use the results from your **Fair-Compare**™ **Agent Satisfaction Benchmark** to:

Promote Your Contact Center as an Employer-of-Choice!

5. Contact Center Assessment

Dr. Jon Anton directs an on-site, in-depth assessment. Result is a 100+ page, point-by-point report on all key performance indicators, complete with color graphics. Can be performed on a collaborative basis with the client's consultants.

Recommended for: Cost and performance-minded managers who:

- want a baseline status (especially if new to the job)

- desire a serious analysis of operational performance and financial impact (ROI and EPS)

- are considering outsourcing (cost-benefit analysis)

- require qualified due diligence assistance in mergers and acquisitions.

Contact Center Assessment

Benchmark Portal "A Datamart of Best Practices"

6. Contact Center Site Certification

Managements who want their centers to be certified as best-in-class have urged us to develop this program, which utilizes our database, expertise and proprietary performance indices.

Recommended for:

- Best practices organizations

- Outsourcers

- Overseas operations of U.S. based organizations

7. AT&T College of Call Center Excellence

AT&T College of Call Center Excellence provides training courses that result in certification of personnel.  Courseware is available for managers, supervisors and agents. Courses are taught both in-person and online. Some courses are in conjunction with BenchmarkPortal industry partners.

Recommended for: All centers. Training is a budget item for all centers that is rarely optimized. We can help you to get more for your training dollar.

8. Benchmarking 201: Your Competitive Edge

This NEW hands-on workshop is for all call center professionals who need a sound benchmark methodology to audit current performance results, then prioritize solutions toward achieving a competitive ROI. Participants will calculate the cause/cost of poor/excessive performance by case studies and quantify a 30-day impact plan. Attendees earn Certification as a Benchmark Specialist through Purdue University's Center for Customer-Driven Quality.

What Will I Learn?

- **Benchmarking the Difference**: Satisfaction, Retention, Operations, Cost containment

- **Competitive Performance**: Peer Reports, Gap analysis on effective/efficiency metrics

- **Solutions Savings**: Root Cause impact, Simulation charts, quantifiable action plan

Recommended for those who need a Peer-Industry Benchmark